Sacred Geography

and the

Paths of the Sun

Sunset at Castel del Monte

Mahmoud Shelton

*Sacred Geography
and the
Paths of the Sun*

Temple of Justice Books

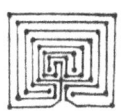

Copyright © 2021 D.M. Shelton

All rights reserved. This book or any portion thereof may not be reproduced or used in any manner whatsoever without the express written permission of the publisher.

templeofjustice@icloud.com

Printed in the United States of America
by Lightning Source Inc.

ISBN 978-0-9741468-3-6

Cover and figures 2 through 8 by B.A.B.
Figure 1 and photographs on pages 2, 20, 53, 66 and 78 courtesy of Shutterstock

Also from Temple of Justice Books:

Alchemy in Middle-earth:
The Significance of J.R.R. Tolkien's
The Lord of the Rings
2003

The Red and the White:
Perspectives on America and the
Primordial Tradition
2019

Mysteries of Dune:
Sufism, Psychedelics, and the Prediction
of Frank Herbert
2020

Contents

List of Figures		6
1	Mysterious Alignments	9
2	The Pythian Apollo	21
3	Metatron	31
4	Harmonia Mundi	43
5	Substitutes of Rome	54
6	The Baptized Sultan	67
7	Lands of the Sun	79
8	The Balance of Britain	92
9	Renewal	105
10	The Imperial Triangle	118
Index of Names		132

List of Figures

1	Heptagram of planets and days	11
2	Relevant points along the axis	17
3	Harmonic locations on the chord	50
4	At the midpoint of the axis	65
5	Orientation of the Castel del Monte	72
6	British alignments on 8 May	93
7	The Seven Spiritual Centers	98
8	The Imperial Triangle	125
9	The Mountain and the Cave	129

> Ask me about the paths of Heaven,
> Since I know them better
> Than the paths of the Earth.
>
> Shah-i Mardan

I will not cease from Mental Fight,
Nor shall my Sword sleep in my hand:
Till we have built Jerusalem,
In Englands green & pleasant Land.

William Blake
"And did those feet in ancient time"

Portrait of John Michell by Maxwell A. Armfield, 1972

1

Mysterious Alignments

The meaning of "science" is knowledge, and the word still holds this significance, although the domain of this knowledge has come to be restricted to the material, or physical, world. This reduction in what may be regarded as truly knowable accompanied the Cartesian reduction of the human being into mind and body, with the power of knowing being considered as somehow less real than what may be measured by it. This reduction constitutes, of course, a betrayal against the earlier understanding of the human being as having a spiritual, psychic, and physical composition. Even more significantly, the materialistic perspective inverts the earlier understanding of matter as having the lowest or coarsest degree of reality. In fact, the physical world itself was understood to partake in reality precisely due to its dependence upon the higher psychic and spiritual degrees. Consequently, traditional sciences were not restricted to the physical domain, and if science was focused on the phenomena of this world, the presence of superior principles was not lost sight of. Of course, science now is synonymous with the manipulation of matter for mundane purposes, and the ugliness and horrors created by modern humanity are no doubt the result of the rejection and ignorance of these superior principles.

Nevertheless, modern humanity has inherited from the traditional sciences an example as commonplace as the seven-day week. Each day of the week is not considered the same as another, despite the equivalence of the quantitative measurement of time. The names used in the Western world for each day betray, in fact, a subtle system of correspondences with superior principles. In particular, each day corresponds to one of the seven planets of Ptolemaic cosmology, and so Sunday is named for the Sun, Monday for the Moon, and so on; and when the English name may have obscured this correspondence, other languages have not, and so in French, for example, the name for Tuesday relates directly to Mars (Mardi) and the name for Wednesday to Mercury (Mercredi). Keeping in mind the Ptolemaic structure of the cosmos, it will be observed that the sequence of days in a week does not follow the proper planetary order in either an ascending or descending manner. There is, however, a geometric way to demonstrate the daily sequence that is so widely followed. In relation to the order of planets positioned in a circle, the sequence of corresponding days traces a heptagram, as is shown in figure 1.

As recently as the Renaissance, the planets were understood to relate specifically to the soul, or rather the psychic domain; the seven liberal arts, for example, by means of which the soul was educated, were likewise related to the planets. Yet it may also be observed that the planets themselves (other than the Sun and Moon) were named for the Roman pantheon. Curiously, the English names of the days that do not relate to the planetary names arise rather from the Norse pantheon, and yet these Norse deities nevertheless are the precise counterparts of the Roman examples: Tuesday is named for Tyr who was identified with Mars, and Thursday is named for Thor, the "thunderer," who corresponds to Jupiter with his thunderbolts. Aside from a kind of linguistic confusion, this example demonstrates that it is not only the planets that are being referenced, but above all their divine namesakes; and so the psychic and

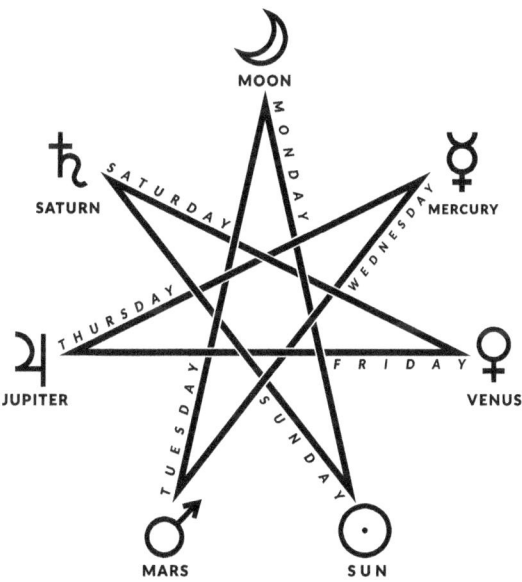

Figure 1
Heptagram of planets and days of the week

spiritual domains are both recalled amidst the physical sequence of days. Modern people still adhere to this ordering of time, and their ignorance of the meaning of this order does not mean that it does not exist.

A seven-fold structuring of the world has been inherited in the ordering not only of time but also of space, although the traditional understanding of "climates" has been replaced by the notion of continents. On the Earth itself, there remain physical reminders of sciences that are ill-understood by the modern sciences that have replaced them. Only in recent years have archaeologists begun to recognize that ancient cities in the Americas were laid out in accordance with astrological considerations, since modern science habitually regards the latter as irrelevant as they were important to our predecessors. Earthworks and stone monuments have survived into the modern era from even older times, and discoveries continue to be made; but even regarding the best known of them, Stonehenge in England, experts are baffled, for example, as to why its bluestones had to be transported from the distant mountains of Wales to be erected on the Salisbury Plain. Indeed, anything relating to principles, such as the choice of location for such monuments and so also their function in the landscape, has been lost sight of; and so, according to René Guénon, "those who study the vestiges of ancient civilizations will never be able to understand the true nature and purpose of what they uncover."[1]

The failure of modern science to fully account for the evidence on the land has given rise to "amateur" attempts at explanation. Unfortunately, all attempts to understand ancient evidence are hindered by the simple fact that the ancient sciences are no longer practiced. They have been replaced by others with very different priorities, as we have seen; and lacking a working knowledge of the principles that were formerly so well understood, modern researchers are predictably bound to see things only in terms of the materialism that dominates their milieu.[2] This is so even when the views of researchers seem to be at odds with the scientific establishment.

Nevertheless, there have been some researchers whose apparent sincerity and intelligence have been able to bring some light to the subject of the so-called "Earth mysteries," and first among them was the late John Michell. Throughout his valuable books, his attention

---

[1] "The Cave and the Labyrinth," *Symbols of Sacred Science*, Hillsdale: Sophia Perennis, 2004.
[2] For example, writers of "alternative history" such as Graham Hancock presume an advanced ancient technology akin to the modern one. Given the absence of such technology, the majority of Hancock's peers have resorted to materialistic fantasies of "alien" technology.

was fixed on his native Britain, but this was often augmented with insight gained from a wider view.[3] His study of Stonehenge and other monuments focused on ancient metrics and the significance to be gleaned from relevant numbers and geometry. By emphasizing the qualitative value of number rather than simply its quantitative aspect, his approach was brought very near the teachings of Pythagoras who inspired him.

Another subject upon which he fixed his gaze were the controversial "ley lines." The term was coined by an investigator who preceded Michell, Alfred Watkins, who had sought to understand the alignments of apparent straightness that he had perceived between landmarks and other subtler markers in the English landscape. In his book *The Old Straight Track*, Watkins demonstrates remarkable insight concerning the likely relevance of the Sun's position in relation to these alignments, as well as the presence of such straight lines worldwide. Whereas Watkins imagined a practical utility behind the development of these leys, however, Michell seems to have been the first to suspect an unseen dimension in his inquiry into these alignments, which has led, unfortunately, to subsequent confusion concerning Earth "energies." The energies that Michell posited in the landscape are not the same as those belonging to the geophysics of materialistic science, just as the channels of acupuncture are not to be equated with physical anatomy. Indeed, Michell was on the right track in comparing the landscape science that he sought to understand with the still-understood principles of Feng Shui.[4] According to this Far Eastern geomancy, energy

---

[3] The subjects mentioned here are to be found explored in his most influential work, *The New View Over Atlantis* (San Francisco: Harper & Row, 1983).

[4] Obviously the popular application of Feng Shui to modern man-made environments is not what is meant here, but rather its more ancient use in determining sacred locations in the natural landscape.

(*chi*) was indeed discernible in the landscape; however, only a negative significance was attached to this energy where it was found to be straight. Nevertheless, Michell found in its doctrines a traditional association between the energies in the earth and the dragon, and this provided a key for him to understand the significance of his discoveries in Britain.

Foremost, perhaps, among these discoveries was what he called the "Saint Michael Line," since this alignment ran over a very great distance through sites dedicated to the angelic dragon slayer. Modern skeptics would attribute this alignment of sites to random chance, since any line on a map will happen to link any number of points. However, Michell's discovery proceeded rather from his view of the landscape from atop a hill in Glastonbury, a center of British sacred history where he long resided; moreover, many characteristics of the Saint Michael Line are remarkable indeed. To begin with, the alignment happens to cross the longest extent of land in southern England, and at its approximate midpoint it runs past the entrance of the largest stone circle in the world at Avebury.[5] What is more, two Somerset hills upon which were placed churches of Saint Michael are actually oriented in their contours to the direction of the alignment, and these contours even bear signs of modification. More striking still, the angle of this line's orientation is supposed to approximate the azimuth of sunrise on the cross-quarter day of early May.

This spring festival, of course, was known to the Celts as Beltane, and its importance has been preserved in the popular memory. Folklore insists on the role of the fairy realm in this festival, and in the context of ley lines it is important to consider the so-called "fairy paths" of Celtic folklore that were understood to be straight. Even into

---

[5] In a sense, Avebury marks the natural center of England, since water flows outward from this location to England's various coasts.

modern times, these paths were respected and their obstruction was avoided. Similar beliefs may be observed for the English "corpse roads," and while the transporting of coffins along unobstructed routes seems to be a human concern, the souls of the dead were likewise associated with straight movement, as may be seen by comparing such notions worldwide. Michell concluded that ley lines were "paths of psychic activity, of apparitions, spirits of the dead or fairies,"[6] and so related to a psychic dimension other than the physical. More tangibly, the Christian inheritors of Britain dedicated points upon these alignments to the angelic and therefore spiritual authority of Saint Michael. As a consequence, the physical landscape of Britain may be understood to have been traditionally ordered by knowledge pertaining to both psychic and spiritual dimensions. No wonder, then, that modern science should be so incapable of understanding these matters.

Along with the discovery of the Saint Michael Line of Britain, another alignment at the far end of Europe was being revealed, but the comparable nature of these discoveries was not at first apparent. It began with the researches of Jean Richer concerning the sacred geography of Greece. Lucien Richer later expanded upon his brother's work by extending an initial alignment of sacred sites dedicated to Apollo. In his article on what he called the "Axis of Saint Michael and of Apollo,"[7] he revealed that this alignment extends to the southeast to Mount Carmel in the Holy Land, while to the northwest, it reaches as far as Britain, passing very many sites dedicated, again, to Saint Michael. Even allowing for the pervasiveness of the archangel's patronage in Christian Europe, it is remarkable indeed that this alignment relates

---

[6] John Michell, *The Earth Spirit: Its Ways, Shrines and Mysteries*, Singapore: Thames and Hudson, 1989, page 10. Concerning the fairies as relating to the psychic domain, see *The Red and the White* (Temple of Justice Books, 2019), chapter 3.
[7] *Atlantis*, May-June 1977.

to *both* of his two principal shrines, at Mount Gargano in Italy and at Mont Saint-Michel in France. Among the other lesser churches of Saint Michael, even the English counterpart of Mont Saint-Michel, Saint Michael's Mount in Cornwall, is very near the alignment's trajectory; but it is perhaps enough to recognize that the alignment extends to the Cornish peninsula, since Saint Michael is, in fact, a patron saint of the whole of Cornwall.

Of course, that the iconography of dragon slaying is shared by Apollo and Saint Michael suggests that this alignment is more than arbitrary; and surely its enormous extent warrants consideration. Unfortunately, there has been from the beginning a fascination with extending the line as far as possible and relating as many points as possible to it, but little regard for the principles that might account for its very existence. At the same time, there has been concern for the "precision" of the alignment in relation to specific sites, yet with so many hilltop shrines being considered, it seems reasonable to allow for the natural constraints of topography while recognizing its overall orientation.[8] Lucien Richer offers that this orientation is "a line of consistent bearing with a meridian, a so-called rhumb line, which can be represented on Mercator's projection of the globe by a straight line;" more exactly, the sequence of alignments between sacred sites "form close parallels to create a corridor which could be interpreted mythologically as a sacred pathway." Keeping this in mind, it is still more important to acknowledge that this consistent orientation or axis has a special significance: from the vantage of Mount Carmel, the angle of this axis corresponds to an orientation toward the sunset on the summer solstice. Given the solar orientation claimed for the Saint Michael Line in England, this does not appear accidental. As if to

---

[8] For a good overview of the alignment in terms of accuracy and probability, see Lukas Mandelbaum, *The Axis of Mithras: Souls, Salvation, and Shrines Across the Ancient World*, Harran House, 2016.

Mysterious Alignments

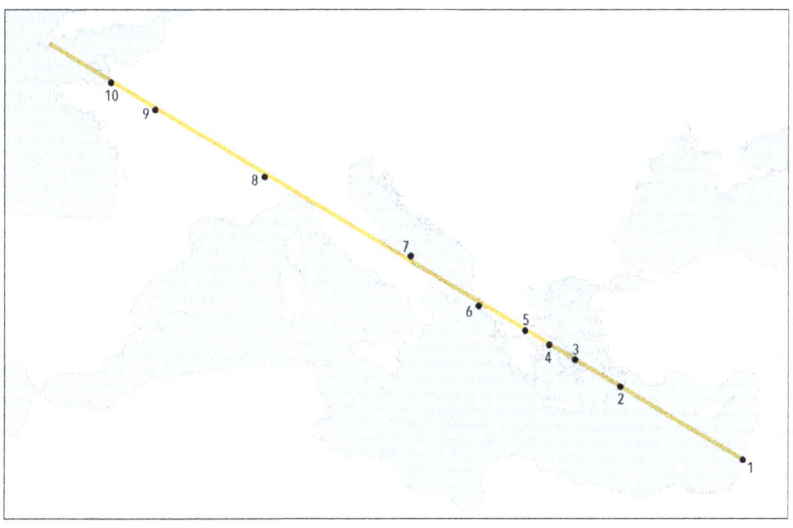

1. Mount Carmel
2. Rhodes
3. Delos
4. Athens
5. Delphi
6. Corfu
7. Mount Gargano
8. Sacra di San Michele
9. Blois
10. Mont Saint-Michel

Figure 2
Relevant points along the axis mentioned in the text

remove any doubt of the alignment's solar relevance, the first land to be reached by following the trajectory from Mount Carmel is the island of Rhodes, best known as the location of one of the Seven Wonders of the Ancient World, the Colossus; and the Colossus of Rhodes was a statue of Helios, the personification of the Sun. Even though the azimuth of the summer solstice shifts slightly with changes in latitude, this variation may also be accounted for by the notion of a "corridor." An approximation of this solar axis or pathway is shown in figure 2.

Following the discovery of these alignments, remarkable efforts have been undertaken by researchers to track the so-called "earth energies" along them on the ground, including the Saint Michael and Apollo Axis throughout its entire length.[9] It is important to recognize that these "energies" were found to be meandering and by no means straight, and that the researchers regarded them as alternatively "male" and "female." Now, the tracking of these energies employed methods of dowsing, and so it is clear that the researchers were dealing with psychic impressions, which may be valid on its level, but this level is not the most important.[10] No doubt the most important considerations would belong to the degree

---

[9] Paul Broadhurst and Hamish Miller published their findings on the Saint Michael Line as *The Sun and the Serpent* in 1989 and *The Dance of the Dragon* on the Saint Michael and Apollo Axis in 2000, both published by Pendragon Press.

[10] Very remarkably, the axis passes the environs of Blois in France, the birthplace of René Guénon who is properly Shaykh Abd al-Wahid Yahya. When the authors turn their attention to Blois, they fail to recognize the spiritual importance of the shaykh, even though Michell was in some measure aware of the importance of the shaykh's legacy (cf. *The Red and the White*, page 17).

above the psychic, and it is that domain that is represented by the Archangel Michael.[11]

Since the axis has such a great extent, it provides a most unusual opportunity to consider the spirituality of different traditions at sites that are bound together in an arrangement that was unperceived until very recently. The same opportunity did not at first emerge with the discovery of the Saint Michael Line, since the spiritual tradition of the Celts remains substantially unknown,[12] despite Michell's insightful observations regarding ancient Britain. We know a great deal more, however, about the Classical traditions of Greece and Rome to which so much of Europe formerly belonged. Even more importantly, with the alignment extending to Mount Carmel, it may be observed that the traditions of Judaism, Christianity, and Islam that are still followed to a greater or lesser degree are in fact linked by this axis. To understand it, we must follow its disregard for the separation of Britain from Europe, or for any national borderline, in favor of other concerns. No doubt spirituality leaves its traces upon history and legend, but whether the traditions are ancient or living, spirituality by definition belongs to a realm above the limits of history; and so by focusing attention on the spiritual traces in this landscape, we are not only investigating the past of the Western world, but very likely its present and future.

---

[11] Obviously, considerations of gender are irrelevant in the example of the spiritual patronage of an angel; often enough, they are irrelevant to the discussion of spirituality. According to the Greatest Master of Islamic esoterism, Ibn `Arabi: "There is no spiritual quality belonging to men to which women do not have equal access."

[12] See ibid., page 22.

The ruins of the Delphic Temple of Apollo at sunset

2

The Pythian Apollo

In Greece, Jean Richer discovered the alignment of sites sacred to Apollo following a visionary dream of Athens.[1] His initial observation linked the birthplace of Apollo, Delos, with his principal shrine at Delphi through Athens. For the Greeks, Delphi was the center of the world, established by Zeus who had released a pair of eagles to the east and west that came to meet at this site near Mount Parnassus. To mark the center, Zeus sent down the Omphalos, or Navel Stone, that was the very stone that had been devoured in Zeus' stead by his father Kronos. In *The Red and the White*, attention was drawn to the correspondences between Kronos and the prophet Abraham, including how a stone sent down from the Heavens is associated with both.[2] For now, we should at least recall that the installation of the Abrahamic Black Stone in Mecca marked the city as the "Navel of the World" (*surat ul-ard*), and so Delphi with its Omphalos partakes in the same symbolism that characterizes a center of sacred geography.

---

[1] See the overview of Richer's work in John Michell and Christine Rhone, *Twelve-Tribe Nations and the Science of Enchanting the Landscape*, London: Thames and Hudson, 1991, pages 97-8.

[2] See chapter 6. It is perhaps worth noting that the name "Parnassus" meaning "Divine House" holds a comparable significance to "betyl," the Greek word for a sacred stone, and "*baytullah*," an Arabic name for the temple in Mecca.

That the center at Delphi should belong to Apollo indicates his central role in the tradition of ancient Greece; and just as a multitude of points may be related to a singular center, so was Apollo known by a great number of epithets. Above all he was Phoebus Apollo or "Bright" Apollo, and although he was identified with light, there is a distinction to be made between Apollo and the Sun, which was personified as Helios, even if Apollo popularly came to subsume the role of the latter. His more essential role was as the patron of archery and of healing, and so also of healing springs.[3] His principal attributes were the bow and the lyre, since he was also the patron of music. In both his healing and musical aspects, then, he was associated with harmony, since a heathy constitution is understood to be harmonious. Along with the use of seven notes in music, it should be observed that the lyre of Apollo had seven strings, and indeed he seems to have been consistently associated with this number. The seventh of the month Bysios, for example, was regarded as the day of his birth, and so it became the time for celebrating his festival.

As Manticus, Apollo was venerated as a prophet, and so he safeguarded the prophecies delivered through the oracles of ancient Greece. Foremost among these oracles was that of Delphi. The site was known also as Pytho, and so the oracle was known as Pythia, and Apollo also as the Pythian Apollo. The Pythia delivered her oracles from atop a tripod positioned over a cleft in the earth, and Plutarch relates that the oracular powers of the Pythia were derived from vapors rising through the cleft from spring waters underneath.[4] Sometimes the Pythia was

---

[3] The veneration of Apollo extended to the Celts, among whom he was known as Belenus ("Bright") and, in relation to thermal springs, Grannus.

[4] Recent research has in fact confirmed the presence of a vapor spring at the site in ancient times, although it is no longer active (De Boer et al., "New Evidence for the Geological Origins of the Ancient Delphic Oracle (Greece)," *Geology*, volume 29 number

The Pythian Apollo

called a bee, since Apollo's gift of prophecy was linked to the bee nymphs who were associated with one of the several sacred springs upon Mount Parnassus.[5] There seems, however, to have been an oracle at Delphi prior to that of Apollo; at least there had been another power there, the dragon named Python, and it is from this name that the name Pytho was derived. The Python was regarded as the child of Gaia, the Earth, and so its chthonic identity is clear. From its home on Mount Parnassus, its function had been to guard the center of the Earth before the arrival of Apollo. Reaching Delphi on foot from the Vale of Tempe in the north, Apollo slays the Python with his arrows, and so Delphi becomes the center of the Mysteries of Apollo.

In *Mysteries of Dune*, attention was given to the association of underworld serpents or dragons with the psychic domain between the spiritual and physical. A. J. Wensinck has considered the symbolism of the underworld dragon in the context of the navel of the world, and so includes material relating to the Ka`ba in Mecca.[6] According to Arab historians, a dragon had lived at that site as its guardian for some 500 years, but that immediately prior to the advent of Islam and the renewal of the Abrahamic temple, a bird "larger than an eagle" dispatched the dragon to a ravine in the adjacent hill of Ajyad. In his illuminating study on *La doctrine initiatique de la pèlerinage*, Charles-André Gilis explains that the dragon and the bird "represent in effect the domain of subtle manifestation and that of spiritual or informal

---

8, August 2008). Its discovery was attributed by Greek historians to a goatherd, who had followed one of his goats into the earth and found his awareness expanded to include the past and future.

[5] It is worth noting in this connection that the Arabic word for prophetic inspiration, *wahy*, is applied to the bee in the Qur'an (XVI, 68).

[6] See *The Ideas of the Western Semites Concerning the Navel of the Earth*, Müler, 1916, pages 63-5.

manifestation respectively." The victory of the latter over the former corresponds to "a purification of the support called to become the center of the new tradition – or more exactly of the power that remains attached to that support."[7] The comparison with the purification of Delphi is obvious enough, and while the dragon guardian is not slain in the Arab accounts, the continued use of the name "Pythia" indicates not merely a commemoration, but rather a survival of function. Just as the underworld serpent or dragon represents the intermediary psychic domain, so the Pythia was positioned between the human world and the decrees of the divine.

As for the spiritual symbolism of the bird, it is by no means absent at Delphi, since according to Pausanias. the eagles of Zeus were represented in decorations attached to the Omphalos. What is more, Apollo himself was believed to appear to mortals in the guise of a hawk. Between the bird in Mecca, the eagles of Zeus, and the hawk of Apollo there is no doubt a shared symbolism, and the distinction of size reflects only a matter of spiritual degree. Apollo is also associated with the crow, but above all he is associated with the swan, a bird with a neck that recalls the serpent. The miraculous chariot of Apollo was believed to be drawn by swans, with his visits to the distant Hyperboreans accomplished by means of this vehicle. According to Pausanias, the Delphic oracle had been established by the Hyperboreans, though no less than four successive temples had been built on the site. The second of these temples was built by the Hyperboreans themselves, and constructed, remarkably, of swan feathers and beeswax.

---

[7] Paris: Les Editions de l'Œvre, 1982, page 98. On page 97, Gilis mentions the dragon as having the face of a goat, a detail he then relates to the Arabic name for the Pole Star at the center of the sky. A correspondence with the discovery of the Delphic spring should be noted. For that matter, it should be recalled that there remains at the Meccan temple a spring no less miraculous than the one formerly at Delphi, the spring of Zamzam.

The Pythian Apollo

The relationship between Apollo and the Hyperboreans is of primary importance in evaluating his function. For Hesiod, the Hyperboreans are the people of the Golden Age. Now, the Golden Age is that ruled by Kronos, and René Guénon draws attention to the formulation of Apollo as Karneios in order to make an important observation.[8] The names Kronos and Karneios are essentially synonymous; the memory of Kronos, however, is dominated by a malefic aspect, whereas Apollo Karneios maintains a beneficent link to the Age of Kronos. The same could be insisted for the northern direction, since "hyperborean" refers to a paradisal aspect quite unlike the malefic north wind. Hesiod relates that with the close of the Golden Age, its people were hidden within the earth to serve as spirit guardians, yet histories indicate a more tangible presence. Leto, the mother of Apollo and Artemis, was said to have been born in Hyperborea. The island of Delos where she gave birth to the twins was, according to Herodotus, distinguished by specifically Hyperborean shrines, and he describes the gifts sent to Delos from the far north through the intermediary of barbarian tribes.

Accounts vary as to the frequency and duration of Apollo's visits to Hyperborea. Diodorus of Sicily mentions the figure of 19 years, and he was well aware of the astronomical significance of this number, since it is the duration of the Metonic cycle that was the foundation of the ancient Greek calendar. Alternatively, the sojourn may have been annual, with the return of Apollo from the north celebrated on the summer solstice; but here again the notion of an astronomical cycle is present. Diodorus also indicates that there was a "spherical" temple of Apollo in Hyperborea, but attempts to find a northern

---

[8] "The Symbolism of Horns," op. cit., 2004.

land beyond the reach of winter in mundane geography have proven futile.[9]

Again, Delos and Delphi define the alignment originally envisioned by Jean Richer. Since these sites are also bound together through their sanctification by the Hyperboreans, the alignment itself suggests an extension of a Hyperborean influence. For René Guénon, Hyperborea is among the names of the supreme spiritual center of the Primordial Tradition.[10] He mentions other names by which the supreme center has been known, such as Tula, or the primeval Syria that is the original Land of the Sun; yet these names have also been applied to centers of a secondary character, to indicate their bond with the supreme center. Despite its insufficiencies, the name Hyperborea at least has the advantage of unmistakably indicating a northern orientation, since the Hyperborean tradition is characterized by a polar emphasis, and so is distinguished from the subsequent tradition derived from it – and that Guénon identifies as "Atlantean" - that is marked by a western orientation and an emphasis on solar symbolism.

In the person of Apollo, while his Hyperborean authority is clear, his solar aspect is likewise unmistakable, hence the assimilation of Apollo to Helios. Here, then, is an example of Guénon's "fusion of forms previously differentiated to give birth to other forms adapted to new circumstances of time and place" that I addressed in *The Red and the White*.[11] The seven-fold

---

[9] For example, it has been suggested that this temple of Apollo is Stonehenge in Britain, but Diodorus did not describe Britain as Hyperborea.

[10] See for example "Atlantis and Hyperborea" in *Traditional Forms and Cosmic Cycles* (Hillsdale: Sophia Perennis, 2003).

[11] Op. cit., quotation on page 22. No doubt the Greek sources concerning the Hyperborean "spirits in the earth," their paradisal northern homeland, and their consecration of shrines should be compared to the memory of the "Ancient White

attributes of Apollo recall the relationship of Ursa Major to the Pole Star that dominates the northern sky;[12] yet he also belongs to the Olympian company of 12, which of course in its zodiacal expression may be understood to be a solar number.[13] Still, the solar character of Apollo was but an aspect of an authority that proceeded from the north and that renewed the tradition of the Greeks.

The legacy of the esoteric Mysteries of Apollo was profound, and this spiritual legacy informed, as Guénon has indicated,[14] the teachings of Pythagoras and Plato. Plato in his *Cratylus* considers that the name "Apollo" indicates his directing of the harmony of the spheres, and this no doubt relates to his polar function. Regarding Pythagoras, his very name indicates his allegiance to the Pythian Apollo, and he was even considered to have been his son. According to Diogenes Laertius, Pythagoras' students believed that he was Apollo himself returned from Hyperborea. Among the characteristics of Pythagoras were his wide travels, and Porphyry relates that he came to Delphi to visit the tomb of Apollo and found it beneath a place called "the tripod."

The tripod is thus a recurring motif at Delphi. The image of the tripod figures in iconography, and in particular with depictions of a dolphin and octopus. The presence of the dolphin may be explained by the very name "Delphi" that refers to the sea creature, since the Homeric Hymns include an account of Apollo's appearance as a dolphin to guide a ship of pilgrims to the new oracle. The octopus, however, is not so easily

---

People" of the American Indian tradition that is the subject of that work.

[12] For this reason, the word "septentrional" is applied to the northern direction.

[13] 7 is the sum of 3 and 4, while 12 is a further elaboration of these numbers through multiplication.

[14] See "Know Thyself" in *Miscellanea*, Hillsdale: Sophia Perennis, 2003. Again, John Michell was himself inspired by Plato and Pythagoras especially.

accounted for. Fortunately, René Guénon identifies the pairing of these symbols in the context of the Pythagorean symbolism of the solstices, a subject he explores in considerable depth.[15] For now what concerns us is the identification of the dolphin as an emblem of Capricorn, and so of the winter solstice, and the octopus as that of Cancer, and so of the summer solstice. However, there is an obstacle to our understanding in that the dolphin, the animal specifically linked to Apollo, is not associated here with the summer solstice, when the Sun reaches its furthest northern extent and when we might imagine an association with the northern location of Hyperborea. Indeed, Guénon explains that it is rather the winter solstice that is associated with the north, since the Sun reverses its course to ascend northwards at that time. This distinction in fact may account for Apollo's aforementioned return *to* the south from Hyperborea on the summer solstice. Our teacher in these matters further explains that for the Pythagoreans, the solstices are in fact "gateways" in the year by which souls were thought to enter or exit this world. Since the winter solstice is understood to allow passage only for a spiritual elect, it is known as a "gate of the gods," with the "gate of men" of the summer solstice being for all others. Even so, it is only in comparison with the spiritual realization of the blessed on the winter solstice that the summer solstice is associated with the malefic aspect of the octopus. With the multiple arms of the octopus indicating a realm of multiplicity, the summer solstice may therefore be

---

[15] See the series of articles collected under the heading "The Symbolism of the Forms of the Cosmos" in *Symbols of Sacred Science*. Jean Richer, appropriately enough, quotes from this material in his *Sacred Geography of the Ancient Greeks* (Albany: SUNY, 1994); unfortunately, in his complicated positing of lines, he mistakenly positions the verticality of the World Axis (*axis mundi*) upon the horizontal dimension of the Earth. Such an axis at the Delphic center may only be represented as a point on a two-dimensional map.

especially associated with the psychic domain, and so also the Underworld, rather than the spiritual world.[16]

In any case, the foregoing should be sufficient to allow us to consider a remarkable implication relating to Jean Richer's discovery. If the angle of the line linking the sites of Apollo approximates the azimuth of sunset on the summer solstice, then it is also true that the same alignment viewed from the opposite direction would be the orientation toward the winter solstice sunrise. The orientation of the alignment passing the environs of Delphi, then, is in perfect keeping with the solsticial symbolism of the dolphin and octopus. The iconography of Delphi therefore suggests an awareness of this alignment and an understanding of its significance. Even the legend of the eagles of Zeus meeting at Delphi from the east and west – and the eagle is the solar animal *par excellence* - likely refers to the presence of this solar corridor. Despite our prolonged ignorance of its very existence, this "sacred pathway" nonetheless appears to very much belong to the sacred sciences of the past. What is more, it is in keeping with the interpretation of ley lines as routes for the "spirits of the dead," since an alignment towards the solsticial gateways in the context of Delphi could only relate to the destiny of the soul.

Of course, the temple of Delphi has long been a ruin, but even after its historical decline, its importance was well understood by the Roman Emperor Constantine when he relocated a relic of the temple to the hippodrome of his new capital in the 4th century CE. This relic was the so-called Serpent Column, the form of which recalls at once the monstrous Python as well as the tripods of Delphi, since there were formerly three heads atop the column. The link with the Pythian Apollo was not limited to providing the Serpent Column with a place of honor in

---

[16] No doubt this characterization is the reason for the temporal setting of Shakespeare's *A Midsummer Night's Dream*, since its plot concerns so explicitly the intermediary realm of fairies.

East Rome, however. Even more revealing is the depiction of the Emperor upon the city's most conspicuous landmark, the Column of Constantine that commemorates the city's dedication, since the emperor is depicted there in the raiment of Apollo.

3

Metatron

While the rise of Rome may have preserved the memory of Apollo, the formulation of Sol Invictus obscured the distinction between Helios and Apollo. There was another figure identified with Helios in the Classical world, however, whose unique role in the Roman Mysteries may indeed be compared with the spiritual role of Apollo as it was understood by the Greeks. This figure was known as Mithras, whose solar character is indicated by the numerical value of his name – 365 – according to Greek gematria. Roman Mithraism has long resisted clarification by modern scholarship, which is not surprising, since the domain of the mysteries is esoteric and therefore its reason for being is beyond the domain of secular science. For example, the relationship of the Roman Mithras with the Mithra of Persia and India is by no means clear. Despite the coincidence of names, however, it should be recognized that through the unusual spelling "Mithras," not only is the gematria significant, but the number of letters is brought to seven. This is not accidental, since like Apollo and unlike Helios, seven seems to be an essential characteristic of Mithras. Initiates into the Mithraic Mysteries followed a path of ascent that was comprised of seven stages, with each rank corresponding to one of the seven planets.¹ The Roman Emperor Julian called Mithras the "seven-rayed god."

In keeping with this esoteric character, initiates gathered in a temple that was either a cave, or a space designed to resemble one. In the first centuries CE, these Mithraea were very numerous throughout the western Roman Empire and have been found even at its very limit in Britain, ² and so an elaborate iconography of its mysteries has been glimpsed through archeology. Recurring images include the birth of Mithras from a rock, and the so-called "water miracle" that shows the appearance of spring water by the shooting of Mithras' arrow; the former recalls the significance of "omphalos" as "navel," while the latter recalls Apollo's association with archery as well as springs.³ The most common image in the Mithraea, however, is very unique, and depicts Mithras in flowing cape and Phrygian cap slaying a bull, surrounded by a consistent assembly of animals and human figures. There is a scholarly consensus that this Tauroctony scene in some manner represents the night sky; after all, in "About the Cave of the Nymphs in the Odyssey," Porphyry had attested to the stellar context of Mithraism. There is disagreement, however, on the matter of how literally the Tauroctony functions as a star chart.

---

[1] The emblem of the first stage of Mithraic initiation was the crow, and so it may be recalled that the crow was sacred to Apollo.

[2] A Mithraic temple was discovered in London in 1954 and attracted great public interest, and so the Mithraic elements in J.R.R. Tolkien's *The Lord of the Rings* that appeared, remarkably enough, in the very same year should not have gone unrecognized; on these elements see *Alchemy in Middle-earth* (Temple of Justice Books, 2003) chapter 2.

[3] The sacredness of archery would not as a rule be preserved in Roman lands beyond the era of Mithraism. On the contrary, archery was honored in the lands of Islam; for example, the Prophet Muhammad is reported to have said: "Archery is a sign and a characteristic among the signs of Islam."

For David Ulansey, who advocates the most literal interpretation, the slaying of the bull – or rather the constellation Taurus - indicates equinoctial precession, or the changing of zodiacal constellations in relation to the spring equinox. Rather than pointing to an identification with the Persian Mithra, the Phrygian caps of Mithras and his torch-bearing attendants prove for Ulansey the importance of the constellation Perseus. In this context, he draws attention to a remarkable quote from the church father Hippolytus: "Perseus is the winged axis which pierces both poles through the center of the earth and rotates the cosmos."[4] Indeed, the polar authority of Mithras easily accounts for another motif in Mithraic iconography, the imagery of Mithras distinct from Sol at banquet and that indicates a greater authority for the former. Here should be seen the meeting of a polar or Hyperborean element with the solar, a matter of no small importance in recognizing the distinction between Mithraism and the veneration of Sol or Helios.

Ulansey also emphasizes the location of Perseus upon the Milky Way, and so quotes Porphyry on the subject of Cancer and Capricorn that Homer calls the "Gates of the Sun:"

> For the Sun advances to these regions, descending from the north to the south and from there ascending to the north. Capricorn and Cancer are close to the Milky Way, occupying its extremities – Cancer to the north and Capricorn to the south. "The land of dreams," according to Pythagoras, is composed of souls, which are gathered to the Milky Way; and the Milky Way is

---

[4] Quoted in Ulansey, *The Origins of the Mithraic Mysteries: Cosmology and Salvation in the Ancient World*, Oxford: Oxford University Press, 1989, page 94. Recall that Perseus like Apollo is a slayer of monsters.

named from the milk with which these are nourished when they have fallen into genesis.⁵

Unfortunately, Ulansey's mechanistic emphasis on equinoctial precession⁶ prevents him from properly appreciating in this regard the significance of Mithras' torch-bearing attendants, despite the fact that Porphyry specifies their positions as being at the north and south. Roger Beck has correctly identified the solsticial significance of the torchbearers Cautes and Cautopates in the context of the Mithreum.⁷ Cautes at the south holds an upturned torch and Cautopates at the north a downturned one, since the southern position of Capricorn relates to the soul's ascent through the "gate of the gods" and the northern position of Cancer relates to the descent through the "gate of men" into "genesis" and multiplicity. In the present context, it is worth observing that these torches are not depicted vertically but rather held at an angle, recalling the angled solsticial alignment of our geographical axis. Be that as it may, these gates belonged to the authority of Mithras in the Roman world, and since Porphyry specifies his proper "seat" to be the celestial equator, his position is balanced between them. Simply put, it was "in the soul's best interest to become a dedicated companion of Mithras,"⁸ for Mithras was a

---

⁵ Quoted in ibid., page 61. Obviously, Porphyry describes the zodiacal signs here in relation to the Sun's relative position in the sky, and not from the perspective of symbolism that belongs to Guénon. The Pythagorean expression "land of dreams" is clearly an appropriate description for an intermediary realm between body and spirit, or waking and sleep.

⁶ In fact, the literal reading of the Tauroctony as a star chart indicates a temporal setting anterior to the Roman era.

⁷ *The religion of the Mithras Cult in the Roman Empire: Mysteries of the Unconquered Sun.* Oxford: Oxford University Press, 2006, pages 107-12.

⁸ E.C. Krupp, "Negotiating the Highwire of Heaven: The Milky Way and the Itinerary of the Soul," *Vistas in Astronomy*, volume 39, issue 4, 1995.

psychopomp, a guide of souls entering and exiting this world.

Due to the presence of these themes in the Mysteries of Mithras, an argument for redefining the Apollo and Saint Michael Axis as an "Axis of Mithras" has been offered by Lukas Mandelbaum in a book so titled.[9] The author unfortunately fails to provide tangible proof of any sort of Mithraic focus upon the alignment. Nevertheless, the presence of Mithraism throughout Europe suggests the pervasiveness of its symbolism on the landscape, even if its mysteries may not assume historical precedence over those of Apollo; after all, the Pythagoreans were already well aware of the solsticial gates. Still, his book is well researched, and full of interesting material. For example, Mandelbaum describes a Mithreum that was designed to allow a beam of sunlight to illuminate its altar on the summer solstice, and he mentions comparable examples of arrangements at other sites.[10] His survey of places in Christian Europe relevant to Roman Mithraism is also of value, and he gives particular attention to the sanctuary at Mount Gargano in Italy.[11]

The sanctuary is the earliest and foremost shrine dedicated to Saint Michael in western Europe. The legendary account of its origin, the *Liber de Apparitione*

---

[9] Op. cit.
[10] Ibid., pages 91-2. Very comparable designs seem to have been perpetuated in Christian Europe. For example, phenomena relating to the summer solstice especially have been discovered at the Imperial palace chapel in Aachen, and a ray of light strikes a unique stone in the floor of Chartres Cathedral at noon on the summer solstice. What is especially remarkable in the latter example is the specific window through which the Sun shines, since it is dedicated to Saint Apollinaris, a name indicating "holy Apollo" (Geoffrey Cornelius and Paul Devereux, *The Secret Language of the Stars and Planets*, San Francisco: Chronicle Books, 1996, pages 164-5).
[11] Pages 104-12.

Sancti Michaelis, dates from the 8th-9th centuries CE, but concerns events purported to begin centuries earlier. The account describes the appearance of the archangel atop the mountain with flaming sword to grant victory to the Christian defenders of Siponto against invading forces. The Feast of the Apparition of Saint Michael commemorates this event on 8 May 663. Framing this history is the supposedly earlier story of the archangel's presence on Mount Gargano, and concerns Saint Michael's intervention to save the life of a bull by reversing the arrow of Garganus, the mountain's namesake, who had sought to punish the wayward animal for taking shelter in a cave. The legend establishes that the cave with its spring is sacred, and the archangel's bond with the site is confirmed by the miraculous imprint of his foot in stone. Mandelbaum observes that the cave, arrow, and bull are all motifs belonging to the Mysteries of Mithra, albeit in different guise. No doubt he is correct in suspecting some sort of renewal for this site. The author, however, considers the miraculous footprint to be a unique element, but in fact it recalls the founding of the Meccan temple associated earlier with Delphi: in the course of constructing the Ka`bah, the prophet Abraham is believed to have left his footprint in stone, and this mark is mentioned in the Holy Qur'an as indicating a place for prayer.[12]

The establishing of the sanctuary at Mount Gargano precedes and prefigures all other more northerly shrines of Saint Michael upon the alignment named for him.[13] For example, legend holds that his other major shrine, that of Mont Saint-Michel in Normandy, was established in 708. No more dramatic location could be imagined, with its

---

[12] II, 125. Cf. *The Red and the White*, page 61.

[13] Saint Francis of Assisi left his mark of the Tau cross in stone at the sanctuary, although it is said that he would not enter the cave, respecting its sanctity. Given the spiritual importance of Saint Francis, it should be noted that Assisi is also upon the Axis of Saint Michael and Apollo.

archetype of a mountain rising as an island above the changing tides of the seacoast. Through the dreams of a local bishop, the archangel is believed to have indicated the shrine's location upon the mountain's peak. A bull and spring likewise figure in its founding, with a stolen bull walking a circle to indicate to the bishop the dimensions of the sanctuary.[14] Traces of the original ground plan of the church may still be seen, despite later constructions of longitudinal design.[15] The dependence of this shrine upon the previous one is demonstrated by the bishop's retrieval of stone from the footprint of Mount Gargano to validate Mont Saint-Michel.

Other sites dedicated to Saint Michael associated with the axis seem to defer to the importance of the two principal shrines. Most remarkably, the foundation of the Sacra di San Michele in Piedmont asserts its position as *Tercium in horum media iustissima positum* ("the third place just lying in the middle of these"), a phrase that seems to confirm its location upon the axis. Also in Italy, the Abbey of Montesiepi traces its founding to a knight named Galgano, who constructs its circular church under the guidance of the Archangel; the similarity of the names Galgano and Gargano is certainly striking.[16] In England, Saint Michael's Mount in Cornwall is understood to be a kind of smaller counterpart of the shrine in Normandy.

A century before Mandelbaum, the story of Mount Gargano had been included in an article by J.J. Modi, "St. Michael of the Christians and Mithra of the Zoroastrians – A Comparison."[17] The author presumes the Roman Mithras to be identical to the Persian Mithra, and

---

[14] Distinct from the example of the goat at Delphi, the bulls would appear to have a solar aspect; after all, the animals sacred to Helios are the Cattle of the Sun.

[15] The reportedly spherical shape of the Hyperborean temple of Apollo should be recalled.

[16] Mandelbaum, pages 46-50.

[17] Papers read before the Anthropological Society of Bombay, Bombay: The British India Press, 1911.

concludes that Persian angelology must have influenced that of the Christians through the figure of Saint Michael. Without referencing Modi directly, René Guénon addresses the comparison of precisely these angelologies in the third chapter of *The King of the World*. He does so in the context of the mysterious Metatron (*Mitatrun* in Arabic) of Abrahamic angelology:

> The etymology of the name *Metatron* is most obscure; among the many hypotheses that have been advanced, one of the most interesting is its derivation from the Chaldean *Mitra*, which means "rain," and which by its root is also sometimes related to "light." Even if this is so, the similarity with the Hindu and Zoroastrian *Mitra* does not constitute a sufficient reason to conclude that it represents a Jewish borrowing from foreign doctrines, for it is not in this wholly external manner that the relationship existing between the different traditions should be envisaged; and we shall say the same concerning the role attributed to rain in almost all traditions, insofar as it is a symbol of the descent of "spiritual influences" from Heaven to Earth.

What especially concerns us here is that he goes on to explain that according to the doctrines of Kabbala, Metatron is explicitly linked to the Archangel Michael (Mikaël):

> "The term *Metatron* conveys the multiple meanings of guardian, lord, messenger, mediator"…we readily say that just as the head of the initiatic hierarchy is the "terrestrial Pole," so *Metatron* is the "celestial Pole;" the latter has his reflection in the former, with whom he stands in direct relation through the "World Axis." "His name is Mikaël, the Great Priest who is both

holocaust and oblation before God. And everything the Israelites do on earth is accomplished according to the archetypes of events in the celestial world. The Great Pontiff here below represents Mikaël, prince of Mercy..."[18]

Guénon does not mention him by name, but the traditional teachings concerning Metatron are clear: "In his earthly incarnation he was the patriarch Enoch,"[19] who is called Idris in Islam. Now, I have already addressed in *The Red and the White* the role of Idris as chief of the spiritual hierarchy and ever-living embodiment of the Hyperborean or Primordial Tradition; moreover, in that work the identification of Idris with the Biblical Melchizedek was explained.[20] With this understood, Guénon's observation concerning Melchizedek is particularly helpful in gaining a fuller view of the spiritual reality that concerns us here: "If we now take *Melki-Tsedek*'s name in its strictest sense, the attributes proper to the 'King of Justice' are the scales and the sword, the same attributes that characterize *Mikaël*, considered as 'Angel of Judgement.'"[21] No doubt the spiritual reality known as Metatron accounts for the relationship between Mithras and Saint Michael, but this reality remains well above the vicissitudes of history. If

---

[18] Hillsdale: Sophia Perennis, 2001, pages 17-8.
[19] Gustave Davidson, *A Dictionary of Angels Including the Fallen Angels*, New York: The Free Press, 1971, page 192.
[20] Pages 31-2. I also mention there that Idris is the patron of geomancers. Geomancy literally means "divination by earth," and in fact may not be so far from an art of the landscape as is supposed. After all, just as geomancy utilizes points and lines, so too we are concerned here with alignments and points on the landscape, and it is especially remarkable that Idris is linked here with Saint Michael, when the latter is so often invoked at the points upon these alignments.
[21] Guénon 2001, page 38.

the patronage of Saint Michael in the course of events came to dominate a landscape formerly marked by the Mysteries of Mithras, this change should be understood as contingent rather than essential.

In keeping with his principal emblems, Saint Michael figures in two principal themes in Christian iconography. His depiction as a "dragon slayer" derives from his war against the dragon in the Biblical Book of Revelation. The archangel also appears weighing the souls of the deceased, demonstrating his role as "lord of souls, conductor and guardian of the spirits of the dead."[22] As the "commander of the celestial militia" in Abrahamic angelology, Saint Michael's spiritual patronage in Christendom extended especially to soldiers, and so to those most aware of the passage from life to death; the parallel with the Roman military's attachment to the Mysteries of Mithras is clear enough. In Christian esoterism, the association of Saint Michael both with the planetary spheres of the Sun and Mercury[23] is perfectly in accord with Islamic teachings, since Idris is above all associated with the Sun that is the Pole and center of the seven spheres;[24] but Idris is also identified with Mercury, or rather his Greek form Hermes, since Idris was the first incarnation of the "Thrice-Great" (*muthallath*) Hermes according to Abu Ma`shar al-Balkhi.

Of course, Hermes like Mithras and Saint Michael is a psychopomp. Moreover, the expression "Thrice-great" has been cited by Roger Beck as also being applied to Mithras, and its meaning may relate to Mithras' flanking

---

[22] Modi, op. cit., page 181.
[23] Amy Hale, "Reigning with Swords of Meteoric Iron: Archangel Michael and the British New Jerusalem," in *The Harp and the Constitution*, Leiden: Brill, 2016, pages 177-8.
[24] The centrality of the Sun is materialistically formulated as heliocentrism, while here its centrality belongs to a geocentric cosmology.

attendants who so resemble him.²⁵ Again according to Islamic esoterism, the rank occupied by Idris at the summit of the spiritual hierarchy is called *Qutb,* or "Pole," and has the numerical value of 111 in gematria. While this number in itself indicates a three-fold unity, the Qutb is also assisted by two Imams, at his right and left,²⁶ and so they are also a group of three. What is especially worth observing now is that one of these Imams is the prophet Elijah or Ilyas, while the solar axis extends in the south to Mount Carmel, an elevation that is known also as the Mountain of Lord Elijah.

---

²⁵ *Beck on Mithraism: Collected Works with New Essays,* Abingdon: Routledge, 2004, pages 134 and 144. The names "Apollo-Mithras-Helios-Hermes" are conflated in examples from Commagene in Anatolia.

²⁶ Just as the two torchbearers of Mithras are associated with the "gate of men" and the "gate of the gods," one of the Imams "watches over the equilibrium of the world" while the other only has "'knowledge of the things of heaven'" (Michel Chodkiewicz, *Seal of the Saints: Prophethood and Sainthood in the Doctrine of Ibn `Arabi,* Cambridge: Islamic Texts Society, 1993, page 96).

Roman copy of a Greek sculpture of Pythagoras

4

Harmonia Mundi

Just as the name of Saint Michael has been attached to hilltops and their shrines in Western Christendom, Saint Elijah seems to have had a similar role in the lands of Orthodox Christianity. It has been presumed that the prevalence of hills named for Saint Elijah represents a development from an earlier solar cult, due to the similarity of the Greek names "Elias" and "Helios," but there is no real evidence for this.[1] These hills, however, do seem to be consistently linked to the practice of praying for rain, which is rather more in keeping with the hagiography of the prophet Elijah.[2] The foremost location associated with this prophet in Judaism, Christianity, and Islam is Mount Carmel, and so its more common name in Arabic is *Jabal Mar Ilyas*, the "Mountain of Lord Elijah." The height is remembered as the location where he resided in his cave, where he built an altar to challenge the worshippers of false gods, and from which he scanned the sky over the sea for rain.[3] Among the many other hills bearing his name, it is no doubt significant that there is a Prophet Elijah Mountain on the island of

---

[1] Cf. F.W. Hasluck, *Christianity and Islam Under the Sultans*, volume I, Oxford: Oxford University Press, 1929, pages 329-30.

[2] Guénon's comment on the significance of rain quoted in the last chapter is no doubt relevant here.

[3] Relevant passages from the Bible may be found in the Book of Kings; for the Islamic understanding of the prophet Elijah, see *The Lore of Light* by Amina Adil, recently republished by Spohr Publishers.

Rhodes, that is the first land reached by following the direction of the summer solstice sunset. Beyond Rhodes the solar corridor reaches to the small island of Nisyros, and again, the highest peak there is likewise known as Prophet Elijah Mountain.

Even so, there is a temple of the Pythian Apollo atop the acropolis of Rhodes. Indeed, the legacy of Apollo has a much greater extent than the alignment between Delos and Delphi. Mention has already been made of the travels of Pythagoras, the "son of Apollo," and it is of great relevance to our subject that his presence at Mount Carmel has been reported, while his tomb is held to be in southern Italy. The author of *The Axis of Mithras* sought in vain for a community who could have been responsible for at least part of the alignment, while Pythagoras is himself present at the origin of the alignment as well as along it at Delphi and reaching like it as far as Italy; and even more importantly, he is our source for the doctrine of the solsticial paths. All that remains of the memory of Pythagoras in the popular imagination is his teachings on the triangle; yet it is important to remember that moderns only consider the physical appearance of things, and that this association with the triangle is not as trivial as they believe. We considered a three-fold symbolism at the end of the last chapter, and it may also be recalled that Pythagoras discovered the tomb of Apollo at Delphi beneath a place called "the tripod:"

> This sacred spot had received its name because it commemorated the spot where Apollo was mourned by the three daughters of a man named Triopas. This place-name may explain the connection, made from later Antiquity into the Renaissance, between Apollo and the triangle. Elsewhere Porphyry says that the triad symbolizes perfection. These pervasive references to the number three connect Porphyry's biographical writings about

Pythagoras with earlier Pythagorean literature concerning the triangle and Plotinus' citing of the triangle as an example of "multiplicity in one"…[4]

René Guénon mentions the Qutb and the two Imams in his article on "A Hieroglyph of the Pole," and explains that the initiatic triangle "must properly be considered as one of the 'signatures' of the Pole."[5]

For Plato, Pythagoras was above all else a teacher of a way of life. Guénon mentions in passing that the Carmelites, whose monastic order was named for Mount Carmel, "link the founding of their order to Elias and to Pythagoras."[6] As is usual in hagiography, accounts of Pythagoras' life include marvelous events, relating to "his ability to hear the music of the spheres (the concordant tones made by the seven planets…as they whirled around the earth) and understand the harmony of the universe."[7]

---

[4] Christiane L. Joost-Gaugier, *Measuring Heaven: Pythagoras and His Influence on Thought and Art in Antiquity and the Middle Ages*, Ithaca: Cornell University Press, 2006, page 49.

[5] Guénon 2004, page 108.

[6] Guénon 2001, page 11. Saint Teresa of Ávila demonstrated the sanctity of Carmelite life, and shortly after her passing was considered for nomination as the patron saint of Spain. She was passed over in favor of Santiago de Compostela, or Saint James the "Moor-killer," whose supposed attribute contrasts completely with the teachings of Saint Teresa that were in special accord with Islamic esoterism, as Miguel Asín Palacios discovered. Now, the pilgrimage route to the supposed relics of Saint James has been likened to the Milky Way, and since the position of the Milky Way relates to the solstices, it is no doubt of interest that the feast day of Saint James is near the summer solstice. However, since the route bears no relation whatsoever to a solsticial alignment, the link to the Milky Way belongs to a realm of imagination independent from any landscape science. The dubious aspects of this pilgrimage are only accentuated by its rising popularity independent from religious concerns.

[7] Joost-Gaugier, page 50.

Indeed, the word *kosmos,* signifying order, was first used by him. The story told of Pythagoras' hearing this harmony concerns a blacksmith's shop, and the tones made by striking hammers of varying size. The same story, remarkably enough, is told much later of the Sufi saint Mevlana Rumi, only the hammering belongs to a goldsmith. This comparison is made more remarkable by acknowledging that the principal rite of the Mevlevi Order, the *Sema* (from the Arabic word for "audition"), is traced to this event, and that this whirling dance is understood to reflect the movement of the planets.[8] For his part, Pythagoras also recommended the practice of dancing. The principal method chosen, however, by Pythagoras to study the harmony of the world was the monochord, a single-stringed instrument that easily demonstrates the relationship between music and mathematics. This instrument allows the user to adjust the length of string by moving its bridge. Harmony appears in relation to the measure of the string; using a monochord, shortening the string by half raises the tone by an "octave," and this word refers to the eighth note after the seven notes of a scale that repeats the tone of the first.

Obviously, the "chord" of "monochord" is a single string; yet in geometry a straight line between two points may likewise be called a chord. An alignment of geographic points may therefore easily be compared to a string, provided the endpoints of the alignment are determined; and this comparison is necessary due to the repeated presence of Pythagoras upon this alignment, whose instrument of choice was a chord. No doubt his notion allows for some interesting observations. Just as a vibrating chord widens in space, it would seem that the influence of the alignment might be extended laterally to

---

[8] The Sema was even practiced upon the Apollo Axis in Athens, in the octagonal Tower of the Winds that served as a lodge for the Whirling Dervishes during the Ottoman period.

account for and encompass apparent geographic "inaccuracies." What is more, it was mentioned before that the dowsers of the Saint Michael and Apollo Axis found on the ground two waves of energy.[9] Without attempting to evaluate the accuracy of their interpretations, their description of these two currents that separate through the landscape and reunite at significant points may easily be compared with waves of vibration that cross at the nodes of a string. Still, while the dowsers pursued the dual forces, the straight line remains a third, balancing term; in this regard, the two "sinuous" waves should be compared with the twin serpents of a caduceus that are balanced on the staff.[10] Of course, the caduceus belongs preeminently to Mercury or Hermes, that is, a form of the Thrice-great Hermes who is principally Idris; and it may be recalled that the caduceus was said to have been a gift from Apollo to Hermes.[11]

As far as the endpoints of this alignment are concerned, we have already presumed them to be Mount Carmel in the south and the Cornish peninsula with its Saint Michael Line in the north. Perhaps the alignment could be extended. Lucien Richer suggested that the axis continues in the north to Skellig Michael off the coast of Ireland, even though the island lacks a solsticial relationship with Mont Saint-Michel and Saint Michael's

---

[9] Broadhurst and Miller, op. cit.

[10] In the microcosmic domain, the caduceus may be compared with the Yogic conception of the three subtle channels, or nadis, and the chakras that are located precisely where they cross. The chakras might therefore be considered akin to the sacred points on the macrocosmic alignment; and since the alignment is being compared to an instrument of sound, it should further be recognized that the force that moves along the axial nadi, the serpentine kundalini, is defined as both luminous and sonorous (cf. René Guénon, "Kundalini Yoga," *Studies in Hinduism*, Hillsdale: Sophia Perennis, 2000).

[11] A caduceus even appears in the hands of a torchbearer in a depiction of Mithras' banquet with Sol found near Rome and now in the Louvre.

Mount; while In the south, Broadhurst and Miller continued their investigations beyond Mount Carmel, but to sites without a solsticial relationship with that height.[12] In the example of the monochord, however, the string must in any case be longer than the positions of the "nut" and "bridge," and the same could be offered for this alignment. With the "bridge" at Mount Carmel, then, and the "nut" at Cornwall, some meaningful proportions appear.

The center of the chord coincides, remarkably enough, with the promontory of Mount Gargano. Conveniently, when the axis is drawn on a map, it follows closely the Adriatic coast of Italy below Gargano, and so the promontory protrudes above the line like the fulcrum of a balance. Here is an example of the shape of the land providentially serving to openly indicate an overlooked mystery. Indeed, much the same claim could be made concerning the headland of Mount Carmel, apparently pointing to indicate movement to the northwest. Be that as it may, the Gargano area holds the balance point of the entire alignment of some 2400 miles.[13] This position may

---

[12] While the trajectory of the alignment seems to continue into empty desert in the south, it should be noted that there are stone monuments there that may very well relate to our subject. Due to developing technology, recent discoveries in these regions have reawakened interest in structures that early aviators marveled at, and that the Bedouin called "Works of the Old Men."

[13] A Mercator projection map allows the axis to be drawn as a straight line, but because of the distention of landforms away from the equator, distances may not be evaluated by such means; for this reason, the midpoint of the axis in figure 1 appears displaced to the north. Conversely, modern computer mapping tools may provide proper distances and therefore proportions, but alignments across the curve of the Earth may not be plotted as straight lines. Incidentally, the matter of the *qiblah*, or proper orientation for a Muslim's prayer, has very similarly been completely confounded by emphasizing quantitative distance over the quality of consistent direction.

Harmonia Mundi

be compared with the "octave" or midpoint of the chord in figure 3.

No doubt the presence of the principal shrine of Saint Michael upon the height adds another significance to his emblem of the scales. As for Apollo, strings figure in both his emblems, the bow and the lyre. The environs of his principal shrine at Delphi are located almost exactly 800 miles from Mount Carmel, so this position represents a third of the total distance. In terms of the monochord, there is no more harmonious relationship to be made with the tone of a string than by shortening the string by a third. For this reason, the resulting tone is called a "perfect" fifth, the number referring not to mathematical proportion, but rather to the fifth note in sequence on a heptatonic scale.[14]

The harmonious placement of Delphi upon the alignment is shown in figure 3, but the significance of this is not yet fully apparent, since it must be considered in light of an ancient enigma at the temple that we have not yet addressed. Visitors to the temple were instructed in part through a display of monumental writings that were attributed to the Seven Sages of Greece. Before reading wisdoms such as "Nothing in excess" and "Know thyself," a pilgrim was confronted with a solitary letter. This capital epsilon or E has the numerical value of 5, but its meaning has always been a mystery. Plutarch offers numerous interpretations in his "About the E at Delphi," and among them he observes that the E has a privileged

---

[14] The story of Delos as his birthplace is especially interesting in the context of a monochord with its moveable bridge. Now, according to the mythology of Apollo, Delos had been a moving island, and was fixed in order for his mother Leto to give birth; its placement was therefore determined with reference to the "god of music." The distance from Mount Carmel to Delos approximates a quarter of our total distance, or half of the distance to the octave as shown in figure 3; a string of such a length produces the fourth of the seven notes in a diatonic scale.

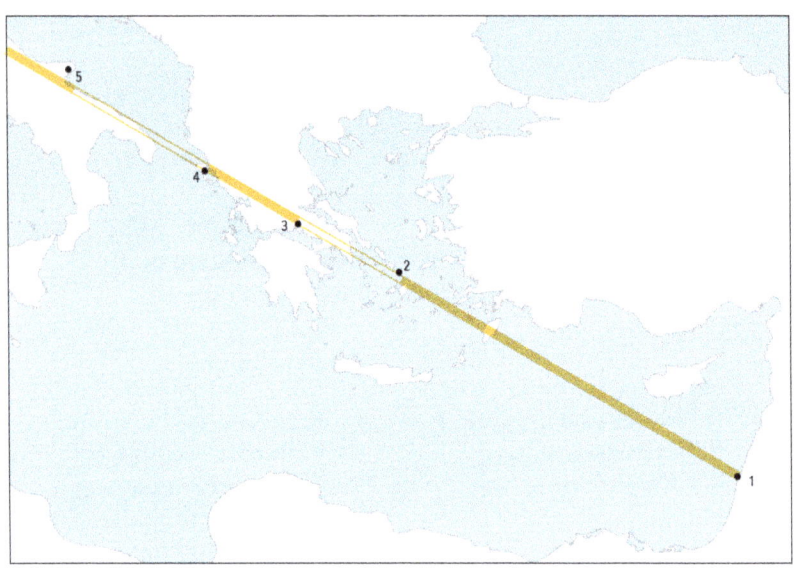

1	Mount Carmel (first)
2	Delos (fourth)
3	Delphi (fifth)
4	Corfu (sixth)
5	Mount Gargano (octave)

Figure 3
Harmonic steps on the chord indicated by segments and corresponding locations

place in musical harmonics. It is not only that musical harmonics are relevant to the temple, however; we may now understand that among other things, this letter is an emblematic declaration of Delphi's special position upon the alignment.

The harmonious relationship of the principal shrines of Saint Michael and of Apollo may assist us further in considering the relationship of their spiritual owners. Obviously a relationship has long been suspected, and explored in academic works such as G.F. Hill's "Apollo and St. Michael: Some Analogies" from 1916.[15] Hill focuses primarily on their shared function against plagues. No doubt healing was a specialty of Saint Michael, and we have already seen Apollo associated with healing springs. Referring to the Celtic form of Apollo, Belen or Belenus, René Guénon confirms that "it is clear that the substitution of the name of the Solar Archangel for that of Belen changes nothing of the sense." This comment was made in relation to Mont Saint-Michel and the nearby Tombelaine, or "Tumulus or Mount of Belen,"[16] and their proximity may very well indicate the relationship that is harmonically expressed by the positions of Mount Gargano and Delphi, especially since the latter is also a "tomb" of Apollo.

The coincidence of Medieval Christian iconographic depictions of Saint Michael with the imagery of Apollo slaying the Python is clear enough, but the source of the Medieval iconography should perhaps be understood. The depiction of the Archangel standing on a serpent seems to appear first in Constantinople's Michaelion, on a painting to celebrate the Emperor Constantine's victory over his enemies. This accords with the notion of the archangel's patronage as "commander of the celestial militia," although the serpent here only figuratively represents the Emperor's enemies. We have already seen

---

[15] *Journal of Hellenic Studies*, volume 36.
[16] "The Land of the Sun," op. cit. 2004.

that the Emperor transferred the Serpent Column of Delphi to his capital and had himself depicted in the likeness of Apollo; the Archangel, then, may very well have been chosen here as a Christian substitute for the slayer of Python.

The pairing of Saint Michael with the dragon is based on a single source, the Book of Revelation, in which the word "dragon," again somewhat figuratively, is used as a formulation of Satan. The dragon is very specifically described in this Biblical source as having seven heads.[17] Despite every symbol having a luminous and tenebrous aspect, there is no allowing in this context for the luminous aspect of the symbolism of the dragon, nor of wishing to see in its use an emblem of "earth energies." Saint Michael embodies the luminous aspect of Metatron, as we have seen; and so his opponent must stand for the "dark face" of Metatron, or rather the "shadow" of Metatron that is cast on inferior degrees of being.[18] Nevertheless, it is important to recognize that no dragon figures in the legends of Mount Gargano, nor is there a dragon involved in the foundation of Mont Saint-Michel.

Even so, the relevance of this "shadow" of Metatron demands that another position along the alignment be considered, a point between Delphi and Mount Gargano: the island of Corfu. Yet this point is not haphazard. Its geographical position some 970 miles from Mount Carmel represents two-fifths of the entire length of our "chord," and so corresponds exactly to the sixth of the seven notes in a diatonic scale. The role of another saint of the Middle Ages intersects the Axis of Saint Michael and of Apollo precisely at Corfu, and the most celebrated legend about this saint concerns his slaying of a seven-headed dragon.

---

[17] 12:3

[18] Guénon 2001, page 19.

Sunset on Corfu, with Saint Spyridon's at left and the Old Fortress

5

Substitutes of Rome

This legend of the slaying of a seven-headed dragon belongs not to Christendom, but rather to Muslim Europe. In particular, it belongs to the Bektashi Order of Sufism and its traditions of Sari Saltik, the saint who above all prefigures the Islamization of the Balkans under the Ottomans.[1] The story that is especially relevant is one related by the consul Alexandre Degrand in his *Souvernirs de la Haute-Albanie* of 1901. Here the dragon is described as "a terrible and immense monster which housed in a cave on the top of a mountain, where it spent the nights. In the daytime, the dragon took up residence in the ruins of a church that it seemed to guard." The hero is described as a venerable old man "dressed in the robes of a dervish and had a long white beard that drooped to his chest. The old man was girded with a wooden sword and bore the branch of a cypress tree in his hand." Upon the mountain, the princess who was being offered in sacrifice to the monster complained of thirst, so "the old man plunged his staff into the cliff and out gushed a spring of water." After the hero slays the dragon by lopping off its seven heads with his wooden sword, he is offered the hand of the princess as reward. Refusing to marry her against her

---

[1] As with the patronage of Saint Michael in Roman Catholic lands and the Mithraism of the Roman military, the Bektashi Order seems to have been especially attached to the Ottoman armed forces; and the Ottomans, of course, understood themselves to be the rightful heirs of East Rome.

will, he asks to live in the dragon's cave instead, and though he dwelled there peacefully, some feared him and began to plot against him.

> A mule then appeared. He mounted it and vanished right through the cliff. When the dervish reached the top of the mountain, he got off the beast and, in four great strides, reached Corfu…Tekkes[2] were built in each of these places where the traces of his footsteps in the stone are objects of great veneration. He is said to have died in Corfu.[3]

Obviously we should acknowledge that the motifs of mountain and cave, miraculous spring and footprint are all likewise present in the legend of Mount Gargano across the Adriatic Sea. Also, like at Delphi, the dragon is a "guard" for "ruins" associated with an earlier religion. There is even a link here with the story of Apollo walking from the Vale of Tempe to reach the center of Delphi, since Corfu now appears as another significant point on the solar alignment reached by foot from the north, and both became destinations for pilgrims venerating the tombs of dragon slayers. Like at Delphi, however, no such tomb remains in evidence on Corfu. Bektashi pilgrims were instead known to visit the tomb of the Christian Saint Spyridon from Cyprus, whose remains were transferred to Corfu when Constantinople was taken by the Ottomans. As aforementioned, Apollo and Saint Michael alike had power over plagues, and the same is attributed to the relics of Saint Spyridon on Corfu.

Frederick Hasluck includes this Albanian tradition regarding Corfu in his monumental study of sacred traditions in Ottoman lands, *Christianity and Islam Under*

---

[2] Dervish lodges
[3] Translations from Robert Elsie, *The Albanian Bektashi: History and Culture of a Dervish Order in the Balkans*, London: I.B. Taurus, 2019, pages 36-8.

the Sultans. In a chapter focusing on Sari Saltik,[4] the author summarizes relevant sections from the incomparable travelogue of the 17th-century savant Evliya Çelebi. This Ottoman pilgrim to places sanctified by saints – his very name "Evliya" means "saints" – encountered a story comparable to the Albanian one at Kaliakra at the other end of the Balkans, on the Bulgarian Black Sea coast. In this example, however, Sari Saltik does not abandon his dragon cave. With his death approaching he calls for seven coffins to be brought, and upon his passing his body is found within each one; the coffins are then sent to various locations as far as Sweden. If the seven-headed dragon embodies the shadow of Metatron, the victory of Sari Saltik over the dragon and his appearance in seven bodies indicates that while we are concerned here with the same symbolism, it is rather the luminous aspect of Metatron that is present.

The hagiography of Sari Saltik has him flying to Kaliakra upon his prayer rug accompanied by Ulu Abdal and Kiçi Abdal, and the names of these companions indicate their spiritual affiliation: the Abdals of Europe, more properly the *Abdal-i Rum* or "Substitutes of Rome."[5] Instead of constituting a proper Sufi order, the Abdals of Rome represent rather a spiritual type indistinguishable from the Kalandars,[6] and played an essential role in the formation of the Ottoman Sufi orders. Among the characteristics of these Abdals was a special attachment

---

[4] Op. cit., page 429-39.

[5] "Rome" in Islam often refers to the historical extent of the Roman Empire, both East and West. The saint Mevlana Rumi is literally "of Rome" and lived in Anatolia; the name for the Ottoman Balkans was Rumelia, the "Land of the Romans." Of course, the axis under consideration reaches a comparable extent through the midst of Roman lands, from Judea to Britain.

[6] Cf. *Mysteries of Dune* (Temple of Justice Books, 2020), chapter 6, especially the warning that those "who took the dress of *qalandaris* in order to indulge in debaucheries are not to be confused with true *qalandaris.*"

to the example of the "Lord of Men" (*shah-i mardan*) `Ali bin Abi Talib, the fourth caliph of the Prophet Muhammad and the first Imam of his holy family. The bifurcated blade of `Ali, Dhul-Fiqar, served as a principle symbol of these dervish warriors, and it is no doubt relevant to our subject that this symbol is considered synonymous with the triangle (*muthallath*), especially the inverted triangle.[7] Along with their spiritual affiliation and physical marks of militancy, the behaviors of the Abdal, or rather their psychic practices, have often enough been classified as unorthodox; such is the case with their use of music.[8] What is more, because of their special attachment to the Shah-i Mardan, the Abdals of Europe are called Alevi and so presumed to be Shiite, which is an unsuitable generalization of this spiritual type, and indeed inconsistent with their historic role in the Balkans. For example, the name of one of the Abdals' most important leaders in the Ottoman period, `Uthman or Otman Baba, demonstrates that this heterodoxy is overstated, since his namesake was the third caliph that Shiism rejects.

In the 15th century account of his life, Otman Baba demonstrates his authority by extinguishing a candle lit by Sari Saltik that had burned for centuries. Like his predecessor, Otman Baba's reach extended to the far north, since he was said to have visited Denmark. His successor, Akyazili Baba, was called the "Second Abraham," while Akyazili Baba's successor, Demir Baba, was a dragon slayer like Sari Saltik. The tombs of these three Abdals in Bulgaria are all monuments of the Ottoman architectural glory of the 16th century CE, yet they are all uniquely distinguished by a heptagonal

---

[7] Emel Esin, "Eren: Les *Derviš* Hétérodoxes Turcs d'Asie Centrale et le Peintre Surnommé 'Siyāh-Kalam,'" *Turcica*, volume 17, 1985, page 21.

[8] Given the importance of the monochord to our subject, it is of interest to note that their practices favored a relatively simple stringed instrument with adjustable frets.

structure that declares like the coffins of Sari Saltik an identification with the number seven. It may also be observed that these tomb complexes have been frequented over the centuries by Christians as well as Muslims, especially on the spring festival of Hidrellez on 6 May.

In his study of *Popular Sufism in Bulgaria and Macedonia*, H.T. Norris translates from stories of Demir Baba, whose proper name was Hasan Pehlivan, in which the Abdal is told by a goatherd:

> "There in the wilds which lie beyond the tumuli, in the valley of the Chermodlanitza river, there, below the rocks, is the 'Five-fingered Spring.' Somewhere, in that locality, will be the site of the tekke of Demir Baba. One day, I lost my nanny-goat and I found her again at that spot…that indicated that this location was a sacred place and that its sanctity would return once more to it." Hasan Pehlivan went to "Five-fingered Spring." He founded his settlement upon the ruins of the ancient monastery of St. George which had been destroyed.

The presence of Demir Baba declares that he "'was the successor to the power and the glory of the ancient master of the valley and the springs.'"[9] Now, the expression "ancient master of the valley and its springs" would seem to be a reference to the so-called "Thracian horseman" of ancient Bulgaria; and while this figure had supposedly been identified by the Christians with Saint George, he had been named in at least some Roman inscriptions as Phoebus, that is, Apollo. Of course, this site would not serve as important a role in history as Delphi; yet with its

---

[9] Abingdon: Routledge, 2006, page 47. In this renewal of a sacred site, even the detail of the lost goat recalls the discovery of the vapor spring at Delphi.

sanctity renewed, we should recognize here a difference only of degree; and instead of Apollo being the renewer, his is the authority in need of renewal in more recent times.

There is no question that the stones of ancient Thracian sanctuaries provided the foundations for many Balkan centers of the Abdal. Despite modern speculation, the ancient rites performed at these sanctuaries are unknown. Yet the same stones serve as tangible supports for the renewed sanctity, and so, for example, visitors to the tombs of the Abdal lie upon prominent monoliths for healing purposes. Modern scholarship is liable to perceive in such examples the persistence of ancient practices in spite of the new religion. This confusion arises from ignorance of the distinction between the psychic and spiritual domains. If we recall the comments of Charles-André Gilis concerning the purification of the "power that remains attached" to a place, we should understand that the knowledge of how to benefit from this power is really a science relating to the psychic domain. This science is often perceived as "shamanistic," and is not foreign to spirituality, but naturally subordinate; indeed, only a truly spiritual presence may ensure the beneficent character of this science and the power with which it is concerned. Of course a flying prayer rug suggests "shamanism," and the weapon of Sari Saltik appears to be the same as "the wooden sword of the shaman and of the Tantric exorcist."[10] What distinguishes the Abdal from others is their spiritual rank, and this is indicated by their very name.

The Prophet Muhammad describes the nature of sainthood in many Traditions (*ahadith*), and the following example mentions the Abdal or "Substitutes" specifically:

---

[10] Emel Esin, "Muhammad Siyah Qalam and the Inner Asian Tradition," *Between China and Iran, Colloquies on Art and Archaeology* 10, New York: Percival David Foundation of Chinese Art, 1985, page 96.

> *The Substitutes in this Community are thirty like Ibrahim the Friend of the Merciful. Every time one of them dies, Allah substitutes another one in his place. By means of them the world turns, you receive rain, and you achieve victory.* [11]

The last sentence in particular should be compared with the authority of Metatron and Saint Michael described earlier, likewise associated with polar symbolism, rain, and military victory. The comparison with Ibrahim in turn recalls the Abdal known as the "Second Abraham," but there is more: the Greatest Master of Islamic esoterism, Muhyiddin Ibn `Arabi, has in fact indicated a relationship between Ibrahim and the Archangel Michael. Shaykh Muhyiddin is also recognized as the "Seal of Muhammadan Sainthood," and according to him, the Abdal in fact number exactly seven. The apparent discrepancy in their number is explained by `Abdur-Rahman Jami, the master of the Naqshbandi Order, who establishes that there are three hundred saints with the power of "loosing and binding," of whom forty are called Abdal; seven of the Abdals occupy the seat of *"Budala'"* (a word composed of the same letters); four of the *Budala'* are called *Awtad*; and the Awtad include the Qutb and his two assistants.[12]

---

[11] Cited in *Islamic Doctrines & Beliefs, volume 1,* translation by Gibril Fouad Haddad, Fenton: As-Sunna Foundation of America, 1999, page 124. The number 40 also figures in the Traditions.

[12] Abu Talib Makki mentions that these three are sometimes called *Athafi*, after the three stones that support a pot over a fire, and this imagery may be compared to the tripods of Delphi. It has been noted that Otman Baba had two Abdals for assistants, Deli Umur and Kaymal (Halil Inalcik, "Dervish and Sultan: An Analysis of the Otman Baba Vilāyetnāmesi," *The Middle East and the Balkans Under the Ottoman Empire*, Bloomington: Indiana University Turkish Studies, 1993).

Modern scholarship prefers to see in the heptagonal architecture of the tombs of the Abdal a show of Shiite heterodoxy, something that the Ottoman state responsible for these masterworks did not tolerate, whereas the seven-fold sainthood of the Abdal was a doctrine, albeit esoteric, that was in perfect harmony with orthodoxy. It has been claimed that "the idea of *kutbiyya* is the basic belief of the radical forms of Islamic Sufi doctrine, in particular in the *kalandariyye* and abdalism;"[13] but what made these forms radical could not have been the "idea" of a spiritual hierarchy, but rather the open assertion that their particular leaders were presiding over it. There is a further link with seven-fold sainthood in the historical expansion of these "radical forms," since they have been traced to a shrine known as the *Yiti Kalandar* or "Seven Kalandars" beyond the Dzungar Gate on the border of China.[14] In fact this shrine is a Central Asian example of a site dedicated to the Companions of the Cave, the saints who are known in Christian sources as the Seven Sleepers of Ephesus; and even though their hagiography is bound up with an emperor of Rome, the shrine in Eastern Turkestan is located near Urumchi, with the etymology of the city's name interpreted as referring to Rum or Rome.

A link to the borders of China is consistent with the hagiography of Sari Saltik according to Evliya Çelebi. Our Ottoman authority explains that Sari Saltik was really named Muhammad Bukhari and was a disciple of Khwaja Ahmad Yesevi of Turkestan, who was widely

---

[13] Inalcik, 1993.
[14] Cf. Emel Esin, "Eren," 1985. Despite the futility of such speculation, modern scholarship is now in agreement that the Hyperborea of the Greeks is linked to the Dzungar Gate and the border of China, which would even for academics trace the authority of Apollo and that of the Abdals to the same source.

regarded as the Qutb of his time.[15] The founder of the Bektashi Order, Hajji Bektash, was likewise considered his disciple. As for the name Sari Saltik, Hasluck relates a strange explanation, that "at Danzig he killed the patriarch 'Svity Nicola,' and, assuming his robes, in this guise made many converts to Islam." Quoting from the original Ottoman source, however, we find the following:

> At Danzig he conversed with Svity Nicola the patriarch, whose name is the same as Sari Saltuk whom he killed, adopted his habit, and by this means converted many thousands to Islam...in Christian countries Sari Saltuk is generally called S. Nicolas, is much revered, and Christian monks ask alms under his auspices.

In any case, it would seem that Evliya Çelebi is providing evidence here to account for an official view of Sari Saltik. In the 16th century, the Ottoman Shaykh of Islam or supreme legal authority Ebu's Su'ud Effendi had issued a fatwa identifying Sari Saltik as a Christian monk who "became a skeleton" by asceticism. This description would then apply to Nicholas, and there seems to be no difficulty here equating this "patriarch" with the very much revered Saint Nicholas, despite the chronological inaccuracy; after all, the spiritual domain is not subject to temporal constraints. Sari Saltik is therefore presented as the spiritual "secret identity" of Saint Nicholas, in a manner that may be compared with the example of Saint Spyridon.

With this mention of Saint Nicholas, we are brought back suddenly to the axis. Like the example of Saint Spyridon on Corfu, the remains of Saint Nicholas were transferred to the Italian city of Bari in 1087; in this case,

---

[15] The name "Muhammad Bukhari" echoes that of the founder of the Naqshbandi Order that more directly descends from the Khwajagan.

however, his bones were in fact stolen. Be that as it may, Bari is positioned precisely upon the axis, in fact rather near its midpoint. The festival of the "Transference of the Relics of Saint Nicholas from Myra to Bari" is celebrated on 9 May, that is, the day after the festival on 8 May of the Apparition of Saint Michael at Gargano; and the chief festival at the sanctuaries of Sari Saltik is 6 May. At Bari, the bones of Saint Nicholas are still involved in what is considered by the faithful an annual miracle, the production of a mysterious water from the bones that is called "manna." In the description of Sari Saltik offered by the Shaykh of Islam, it is curious, then, that Christian bones are specifically mentioned. Likewise curious is the trigonal relationship that may be observed between the locations of Bari and the two principal tombs of Sari Saltik in the western Balkans, atop Mount Kruje in Albania and at the spring of Blagaj in Bosnia; this relationship is demonstrated in figure 4. In fact, since their positions form a perfect equilateral triangle, might we not have here one of the "'signatures' of the Pole?"

A final connection may be of particular significance to these matters. The iconographies of Saint Spyridon and Saint Nicholas alike include a confrontation with the same figure, Arius, at the Council of Nicaea in the 4th century CE. Both are remembered for opposing Arius' theological position, according to which Jesus Christ was considered subordinate to God the Father rather than consubstantial. In the course of the council's rejection of Arius' position, Saint Nicholas is remembered for striking Arius in the face, and there are icons of Saint Spyridon covering his opponent's mouth. As a consequence of Saint Nicholas' action, the Emperor Constantine supposedly revoked his sacerdotal vestment, albeit temporarily. In the 12th century CE, Peter the Venerable disrespectfully characterized the Prophet of Islam as the successor to Arius, so it is not out of keeping with this for a saint of Islam to represent Arianism for the Christian

West, especially if he is wearing the habit of a Christian.[16] What is especially strange, then, is the violence by which Sari Saltik was said to have become Saint Nicholas, since it would appear to belong to a larger scheme of Divine Justice. In the language of the legend of Mount Gargano, the arrow has been turned back against the archer.[17]

---

[16] Note the similarity of letters between the name Arius and the title "Sari."

[17] In the modern West, Saint Nicholas, or rather Santa Claus, retains a rather unique presence. Despite the rejection of saints through stages of antitraditional action, Santa Claus preserves for the popular consciousness a debased formulation of saintly authority; but what must be insisted upon is that two of his most distinctive characteristics, an abode in a Nordic country and his supernatural flight, are easily related to Sari Saltik and not to the Christian saint at all. Just as the exploits of Sari Saltik were understood to have prefigured Ottoman rule in the Balkans, the historical Dracula – whose title means "Dragon" - opposed the Ottomans, and both of these emblematic figures remain archetypal in the popular consciousness.

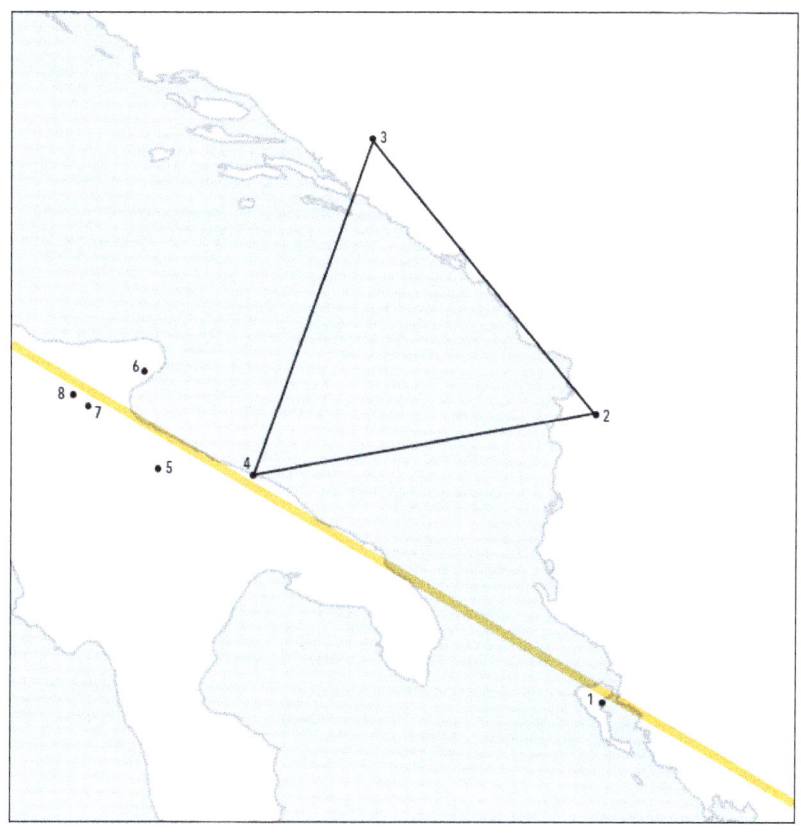

1 Corfu
2 Mount Kruje
3 Blagaj
4 Bari
5 Castel del Monte
6 Mount Gargano
7 Loggia
8 Lucera

Figure 4
At the midpoint of the axis

65

Castel del Monte with its open views to the horizon

6

The Baptized Sultan

Perhaps the most iconic architectural structure at the Sanctuary of the Archangel upon Mount Gargano is the octagonal campanile, built in the 13th century as a watchtower, although it was later converted into a bell tower and reduced in height. We have already noted the presence of an octagonal structure upon the Axis of Apollo, the Tower of the Winds in Athens, and there is no doubt that this monument has served as a prototype for other octagonal towers. Indeed, many copies of this prototype have been built in England and elsewhere, and it is at least curious that its earliest recognized copy, the 15th century Torre del Marzocco in Livorno, happens to be found upon the axis as well. The tower of ancient Athens was properly called the Horologion, and so was principally a clock, although it too was converted into a bell tower during Christian times. Its octagonal design was meant to embody the eight winds of Greek cosmology that belonged to the cardinal directions and to the four directions between them. Thanks to Evliya Çelebi, the same Ottoman traveler who is our source for the personality of Sari Saltik, we also know that the Tower of the Winds originally contained representations of the zodiac and of the planets, as well as 366 talismans. This number reveals, of course, that the tower had a solar emphasis, and this emphasis is in keeping with the solar orientation of the axis. Modern scholarship recognizes the tower as a monument of cosmic order, but its ignored talismanic function suggests that it formerly played a more active role in the preservation of that order.

While the dominance of east and west is obvious in solar considerations, we have seen that the solstices are to the north and south. Since the Sun at the equinoxes is balanced between these extremes, the equinoxes and the solstices in temporal terms should be understood to correspond to the four cardinal directions of space. In positing a terrestrial axis in line with the Sun at its solstices, however, the resulting line forms an angle upon a map that is intermediate to the cardinal directions. What is more, the Festival of the Apparition at Mount Gargano is 8 May, that is, a date midway between the spring equinox and the summer solstice. Conveniently, the octagon is the geometric figure that indicates in space what is marked in time as the solstices, equinoxes, and the four cross-quarter days in-between.

Now, the tomb architecture of the Abdals expresses in its heptagonal form a special spiritual presence, but the octagon should not be confused with it, nor be understood necessarily to indicate a superior degree than the heptagon. As René Guénon has explained in his study of the octagon,[1] its geometry expresses an intermediary rather than a spiritual dimension, as, for example, in the architectural transition from a quadrangular base to a dome. He also mentions the comparable role of the octagonal baptistry in enabling the transition from secular to spiritual space in a church, and how its use constitutes a kind of psychic preparation. While it may be observed that the octagon rather than the heptagon is generally employed in Islamic tomb architecture, this is in perfect accordance with the grave state being intermediate between this world and the next. The octagonal Palatine Chapel in Aachen belonged to the Holy Roman Emperor, and although it was not built as a tomb, its design still relates to an intermediary function,

---

[1] "The Octagon," op. cit. 2004.

since the emperor is traditionally known as *pontifex* or "bridge builder."

The Pythagorean doctrine of the solsticial gates clarifies the nature of the solar corridor as relating to journeys for souls, and so to the psychic domain that is intermediary between the spiritual and corporeal. The octagonal baptistry and its function for the soul has a particular importance to our subject, since the liturgical feast of Saint John the Baptist is assigned to the period of the summer solstice when sunset determines the path of the alignment.[2] Even the Delphic symbol for the summer solstice is the octopus, literally the "eight-footed." It would not be unreasonable, then, to find in the octagonal geometry of the watchtower at the center of the alignment an appropriate emblem of the symbolism under consideration, with even the identity of its builder - a Holy Roman Emperor – conforming to this symbolism. Rather astounding, then, is the placement of a greater octagonal structure very near the alignment built by the same emperor, Frederick II. In the example of this structure, the Castel del Monte, no more elaborate demonstration of octagonal symbolism in architecture has ever been realized anywhere on Earth.

The Castel del Monte has been subject to many arcane interpretations with scant evidence, yet this architectural marvel has apparently never been associated with the Axis of Saint Michael and Apollo. This is not too surprising, given the importance of the sanctuary a short distance to the north at Mount Gargano. Because of this importance, however, it is perhaps overlooked that its position is consistently the furthest from the axis when an attempt is made to bring a proposed alignment as near as

---

[2] Remarkably, the chivalric Order of Saint John had their headquarters upon the alignment, since they occupied the island of Rhodes from 1310 to 1522. For this reason, they are still known as the "Knights of Rhodes."

possible to all significant sites.³ Clearly the sanctuary is found some miles to the north of the axis, and if we are as generous in our allowance of mileage southwards from the alignment to accommodate relevant sites, we are compelled to include the Castel del Monte. The axis at its center may then be seen to pass between the two octagonal monuments erected by the emperor, as is shown in figure 4.

The uniqueness of the Castel del Monte is but a reflection of its builder, Frederick II: "He was the first and only medieval Emperor who drank of the spirit of the East and came home to fuse it with the Holy Roman Empire."⁴ Frederick therefore prefigures the Ottoman rulers in his Islamization of Roman Imperial traditions. As the heir of the Norman kingdom of Sicily, Frederick also embodied an ideal of monarchy that brought together a Germanic heritage with that of the Fatimid caliphate that had ruled Sicily before the Normans. Because of the incorporation of Islamic culture at the court of these Norman kings, Frederick II along with his grandfather Roger II have been called the "two baptized sultans" by historians; and since the Normans are properly "Norse men," the authority of Frederick II in Italy thus embodied a north-south dimension especially.⁵ A contemporary of Saint Francis of

---

³ Cf. the data on page 107 of Michell and Rhone 1991, and Appendix A of Mandelbaum 2016.
⁴ Ernst Kantorowicz, *Frederick the Second 1197-1250*, translated by E.O. Lorimer, New York: Frederick Ungar Publishing, 1957, page 197.
⁵ The complementary relationship of east and west or north and south lends their respective meeting the suggestion of balance. This is expressed very beautifully, for example, in Viking burials that contain sacred Arabic formulae, a fact that makes archaeologists uncomfortable. In Christian terms, it is the Italian Santa Lucia who illuminates the Scandinavian north, and Frederick II passed away on her feast day. In the case of easterners seeking to live in the west, however, they have all too often forgotten that, historically speaking, illumination does not

Assisi, the emperor is remembered primarily for his scientific patronage, and no doubt he served as a pontifex for the sciences of Islam. For example, through the emperor's personal support, the mathematician Fibonacci was able to transmit the use of the zero and the so-called "Fibonacci Sequence" from Islamic civilization. The emperor's scientific interests moreover included those of religion, as evidenced by including among his "Sicilian Questions" an inquiry into the meaning of a spiritual Tradition of the Prophet Muhammad. Even at the time, Frederick II was recognized for his personal approach to the world of Islam. The establishment of the Muslim settlement of Lucera proves his interest in his Muslim subjects, while his own court he established a short distance away in Foggia; and curiously, both towns are in a linear relationship that approximates the solar alignment (see figure 4). Papal authority mocked the emperor as the "Sultan of Lucera" and excommunicated him for his failure to Crusade against Islam. Nevertheless, he succeeded where Crusade failed, becoming ruler in Jerusalem through peaceful and respectful diplomacy.

Even though Frederick II visited the Dome of the Rock, the Castel del Monte that he later constructed was not its copy. The Castel, after all, is not a dome, and in comparing it with other octagonal structures, Heinz Götze in his detailed study of the monument gives only passing mention of the shrine in Jerusalem.[6] Nevertheless, Götze establishes that its design is of indisputably Islamic inspiration. Moreover, the author demonstrates that with its eight octagonal surrounding towers, the core geometry of the Castel del Monte is that of a star, although it is hidden in a sense, albeit in plain sight (this star is depicted in figure 5).

---

come from the west, and they may become overwhelmed by materialism, or worse.

[6] *Castel del Monte: Geometric Marvel of the Middle Ages*, translated by Mary Schäfer, Munich: Prestel, 1998.

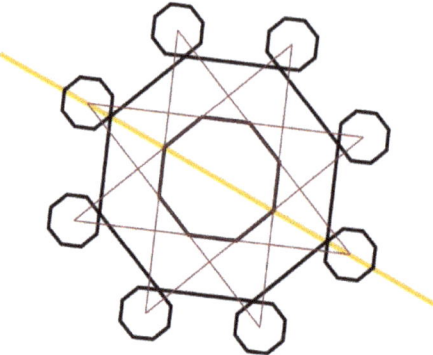

Figure 5
Orientation of the Castel del Monte's geometry (after Götze)

Götze makes some worthwhile speculations concerning its significance, but fails to consider a peculiarity of the monument: its orientation, or rather its apparent lack of one, since the points of the star are not oriented to the cardinal directions. Its entrance faces slightly south of east, but this direction does not correspond to sunrise on any likely Christian festival. However, when the point at the south of the door is connected to its opposite point at the northwest by a line, this line appears to match the angle of the alignment with the solstices (see figure 5).

Stars, and especially the meanings attached to them, are the concern of astrologers, and the emperor's court in Foggia hosted one of the most renowned astrological authorities of any age, Michael Scot. Having left his native Britain for studies abroad, including in Toledo where sciences could be more directly received from the world of Islam, Scot excelled especially in mathematics, and so was known as "Michael Mathematicus." Rather remarkably, given the present subject, he was also known in his time as a "Second Apollo." Perhaps the greatest of his works that he dedicated to Emperor Frederick II, the

Liber introductorius, includes a section on the relationship of music and astronomy and the use of the monochord. In his presentation of correspondences between the seven notes of a scale and the seven planets, he assigns the eighth note, the octave, to the sphere of the fixed stars. Is it coincidence, then, given the specific placement of the shrines of Apollo upon the alignment, that the "Second Apollo" should be linked to the middle of this chord, or octave, and its eight-pointed star?

Among the concerns of the traditional astrologer is the designing of talismans, and since we know that the octagonal Tower of the Winds served a talismanic purpose, it must be allowed that the Castel del Monte might have served a similar purpose. A lack of evidence available to historians is not an argument against this occult[7] interpretation; after all, Scot appears in legends as the wizard of the North, with very occult powers indeed. Sir Walter Scott, his supposed descendant, explains some of these legends in his notes to *The Lay of the Last Minstrel*. He mentions the survival of Scot's magic books, but that they "could not be opened without danger, on account of the fiends who were thereby invoked;" and if even opening the books was an invocation of unseen forces, they would have included talismans that by definition have such forces attached to their designs. By means of his command over "demon" and "fiend", the wizard was held to have split the Eildon Hill in Scotland into three hills, and to have flown from Britain to France on the back of what appeared to be a huge black horse. Scott relates elsewhere another tale told of the Eildon Hills, in which the "Once and Future" King Arthur along with his knights sleep under the earth until the time of his awakening.

Elsewhere I have addressed the insufficiencies of Christian cosmology in accounting for beings belonging

---

[7] The primary meaning of "occult" is not sinister, but rather "hidden."

to a rank intermediate between angels and human beings.[8] At their most generous, Christians have allowed that they are the fairies, and traced them to the "neutral angels" who did not take sides in the war between Saint Michael and the Devil; more commonly, they are dismissed as the demons who were opposed to the archangel. No doubt it is of interest that they are consistently related to Saint Michael. In Islam, however, they are identified as the Jinn, and may be good or evil. In the Holy Qur'an, the prophet-king Solomon is remembered for having command over the Jinn, as well as over the winds on which he flew with his court.[9] Clearly the legend of Michael Scot astride his flying horse recalls both of these Solomonic powers, and no matter the veracity of the legend, Scot was well aware of Solomon's authority in such matters.[10] Given the possibility of a talismanic function in the design of the Castel del Monte, it is at least worth observing that the towers are anchored to the octagon as loops (see figure 5), and that this concept strongly recalls an occult talisman known as the "Footprint of Solomon."

Of course, the position of Frederick II as pontifex between Christendom and Islam could only be viewed as blasphemous by the Church, and Pope Gregory IX went so far as to compare him to "the blasphemous Beast of the Apocalypse" that in the Book of Revelation is associated with the dragon. The distinctive attribute of the Beast, its

---

[8] *The Red and the White*, chapter 3.
[9] XXXIV, 12. According to Islamic esoterism, Solomon is understood to have a special bond with Metatron (Emel Esin, "Turkic and Ilkhanid Universal Monarch Representations and the Cakravartin," *Proceedings of the Twenty-sixth International Congress of Orientalists*, volume II, New Delhi, 1968, page 109), while Pythagoras is considered to be under the authority of the prophet-king.
[10] Charles H. Haskins, "Michael Scot and Frederick II," *Isis*, volume 4 number 2, Chicago: The University of Chicago Press, 1921, page 261.

horns, was specifically invoked in the Cistercians' name for him, *"Fridericus Cornutus."* We have already considered that the dragon of the Apocalypse represents the shadow of Metatron, and René Guénon has explained in "The Symbolism of Horns" that this attribute of the Beast is but a malefic expression of power that may in a different context appear as a sign of legitimacy.[11] Frederic's biographer insightfully considers these horns to be emblematic of the very contrasting views of the emperor that prevailed in his day.[12] Guénon indicates that in Arabic sources Alexander the Great is called Iskandar Dhul-Qarnayn, "that is, 'of the two horns,' which is most frequently interpreted in the sense of a double power extending over both the East and the West." No doubt Frederick II should be recognized as a "Second Alexander" as indeed he was, since this title rightly identifies his role as "the great intermediary and reconciler of East and West."[13]

There is an important point to insist upon here, however. Whereas the meeting of east and west is accomplished in the physical world, and the psychic realm is intermediate between the spiritual and physical, it will be remembered that the meaning of the name "Metatron" is similarly "mediator," although with Metatron there can be no question of a domain other than the spiritual. Through the World Axis, however, the spiritual influence of Metatron extends to the other domains, as we have suggested, and such is the case with Iskandar Dhul-Qarnayn who is regarded in Islam as a prophet, and so also to a lesser degree with the "Second Alexander" by spiritual affinity, given the above considerations. No doubt the reconciliation of Christianity and Islam, such as we have witnessed with

---

[11] Op. cit.
[12] Kantorowicz, page 609.
[13] Ibid., page 192, 494.

Sari Saltik, may only be approached by means of this influence.

In a medieval legend summarized by Julius Evola, Frederick is presented with a gift of three mysterious stones and a question concerning what was best in the world. His answer to the question was, significantly enough, "measure;" but the emperor was judged to be "wise in word but not in deeds because he did not inquire about the most excellent powers of the stones."[14] This legend is clearly related to the story of Alexander and the angels' gift of a "wonder-stone," a *"lapis exilis,"* that when placed on a scale outweighs any amount of gold but is lighter than a handful of earth; in other words, it is a stone than expresses an otherworldly measure. Now, this legend not only confirms his bond with Alexander the Great, but it also suggests a relationship with an angelic measure and so recalls the scales of Saint Michael as well as the alignment named for him. It should not be overlooked, although Evola seems to have done so, that this story of Alexander is likewise a source for the legend of the Grail, or *lapis exillis,* and of the knight who fails to ask the right question.[15]

Ernst Kantorowicz frames his 700-page biography of Frederick II with prophecies of the Classical world, since this Medieval emperor most nearly embodied Virgil's promise of "who shall bring peace on earth and the Age of Gold, and shall evoke once more the kingdom of Apollo."[16] Of his subject, the "Sun King" whose birth and death alike fell within days of the winter solstice, the biographer offers this strange assessment: "From birth his life ran arrow-straight to its zenith, then quitted earth and vanished like a comet in the ether: perchance to reappear

---

[14] *The Mystery of the Grail*, Rochester: Inner Traditions, 1996, page 43.
[15] Cf. Friedrich Ranke, "The Symbolism of the Grail in Wolfram von Eschenbach," *The Grail: A Casebook*, edited by Dhira B. Mahoney, Abingdon: Routledge, 2014, page 372.
[16] Op. cit., page 3.

once more in fiery brilliance at the end of time." The notion of his reappearance is not the author's fancy, however, for upon the passing of Frederick II, there circulated a belief that he was not really dead, but asleep within Mount Etna in Sicily instead. Indeed, at the moment of the emperor's passing, it was said that a Franciscan in prayer had witnessed

> a mighty train of five thousand armed horsemen riding towards the shore and plunging into the sea. Then the sea hissed as if all the riders had been armed in glowing metal, and one of the horsemen said to the astonished monk "that was Kaiser Frederick, riding into Etna with his men."[17]

Such was the testimony concerning Frederick II's intermediary state between worlds, and reminder enough for the monk's contemporaries to repeat the words of a prophecy, *"imperator vivit et non vivit"* ("the emperor lives and does not live"). As far as Mount Etna is concerned, the emperor would seem to have had legendary company. In his *Otia Imperialia* of c. 1211 - some 40 years *before* the passing of Frederick II - Gervase of Tilbury relates how a Sicilian groom had already found none other than King Arthur inside Mount Etna. It is strange, then, to find the perpetual life of Arthur attached both to Frederick II at Mount Etna as well as the wizard Michael Scot at the Eildon Hills, since the solar axis leads like the path of an arrow from their Imperial court to the land of Britain.

---

[17] Ibid., pages 685-7.

The Abbot's Kitchen, the only monastic building to survive the "suppression" of Glastonbury Abbey intact

7

Lands of the Sun

There is another Emperor Frederick said to be sleeping within another mountain, Frederick I Barbarossa in Germany's Kyffhäuser. Kantorowicz has shown, however, how this identification is a later alteration, and that it was in fact Frederick II who had been replaced by his grandfather: "The mountain would to-day stand empty if it were not for the son of Barbarossa's son."[1] Apparently the German people could more easily imagine the more Germanic Frederick as haunting their native landscape, yet here the imagination is deceptive. Only Frederick II as a "Second Alexander" embodies the presence of a mediating principle that alone may be characterized as ever-living, and the same may not be said of the Crusading emperor. There is an accompanying legend in this landscape, that of the "Wild Hunt," in which spectral horsemen are led by the emperor himself across the landscape.[2] Following the course of the solsticial corridor into northwestern France, however, the Wild Hunt is known as *La Chasse Artu,* or the Hunt of Arthur. We have already encountered examples of supernatural horsemen, from the "five thousand" in Sicily to Michael Scot astride his black mount; and the ascension of Elijah in fact provides another example, because Islamic sources prefer a "Horse of Fire" to a

---

[1] Ibid., page 689.
[2] The leader of the Wild Hunt in Germany was also sometimes thought to be Wotan, or the Devil himself.

"Chariot of Fire" for his means of ascension. These examples share another theme, of course, since Elijah, like Emperor Frederick II and King Arthur, is believed to still be alive.

In religious terms, however, the fullest expression of supernatural travel belongs to the "Night Journey and Ascension" of the Prophet of Islam. As the name indicates, this miracle is comprised of two dimensions: the "horizontal" journey of the Prophet Muhammad from Arabia to Jerusalem, mounted upon the otherworldly creature called the Buraq; and his "vertical" ascension to the Divine Presence. It is obviously the journey that concerns us here, and since it is related to have occurred in stages, with the Prophet dismounting in order to pray at especially sacred sites, this travel may be compared to the miraculous travel of Sari Saltik from Albania to Corfu in literal "steps." What is more, there is a footprint in stone at the Dome of the Rock in Jerusalem attributed to the Prophet Muhammad at the meeting place of the miracle's terrestrial and celestial dimensions. In this context, the Arabic word for "journey," *isra'*, is of particular significance. It relates etymologically to the word "secret," *sirr* (plural *asrar*), as well as to the name "Syria," and so it is worth observing that the traditional extent of the geographic region so named includes Jerusalem (as well as Mount Carmel). Mention was made earlier of the name Syria being originally applied to the primeval Hyperborean center, and in his article on the "The Science of Letters (*Ilm al-huruf*)," René Guénon makes some remarkable observations concerning the language of the antediluvian Adam being called in Islamic esoterism the "Syriac language:" "According to the interpretation given to the name, this *lughah suryāniyyah* is properly speaking the language of "solar illumination," *shams ishrāqiyyah*; in fact *Sūryā* is the Sanskrit name of the Sun, and this word seem to indicate that its root, *sur*, one of those designating light, itself belongs to the original language."³ Of course, since the journey of the Prophet of Islam is specifically the "Night Journey," we needn't search for solar aspects relating to his path beyond the Syrian location of the Dome of the Rock.

Elsewhere, in "The Land of the Sun," Guénon focuses on another location as an image of the primeval Syria, Glastonbury in England. Now, it will be recalled that the man who discovered the Saint Michael Line, John Michell,⁴ did so upon a hill overlooking Glastonbury. The occasion for René Guénon to devote an entire article specifically to the sacred geography of Glastonbury arose through the discovery by the artist Katharine Maltwood of the so-called "Glastonbury Zodiac," a giant ring of astrological effigies apparently designed upon the landscape.⁵ The word "discovery" is used here, although a biographer of Doctor John Dee insists that the Elizabethan mage was well acquainted with the effigies.⁶ Regardless, Guénon agrees with Maltwood that the earthworks indicate "an art based on the principles of Geometry," and offers that while the Druids would have

---

³ Guénon 2004. Cf. also chapter 5 note 15 above.

⁴ By now the import of the name "Michell" should be apparent, as itself a link between England and the Normans of France through the remembrance of the angel saint. John Michell's middle name is Frederick.

⁵ "The Land of the Sun" is included in Guénon 2004. Maltwood first presented her discoveries in *A Guide to Glastonbury's Temple of the Stars*, published in 1934, and it is at least worth noting that her musings on the landscape includes a reference to Mount Carmel.

⁶ Richard Deacon, *John Dee: Scientist, Geographer, Astrologer and Secret Agent to Elizabeth I*, London: Frederick Muller, 1968. Dr. Dee used as a kind of signature the delta, the fourth letter of the Greek alphabet that is geometrically a triangle and so an emblem of the union of three and four. In the present context, it is worth recalling that a special concern of Dee was the recovery of the original language of Adam by means of his "Arabic" Book of Soyga.

been involved in their preservation, their origin is no doubt older.[7] He maintains that certain particulars of the zodiac's design are unquestionably Hyperborean, and this evidence marks Glastonbury as an ancient center modelled upon the supreme center of the Primordial Tradition. This last point helps explain why Glastonbury has been conflated with the legendary Avalon, a name that is obviously synonymous with Belen or Ablun, the Celtic Apollo. It is also especially important to observe the etymological link between Belen and the name Beltane, since the Saint Michael Line discovered in Glastonbury apparently coincides with the azimuth of sunrise at the time of this ancient festival.

In light of this mention of Apollo, it is surely significant that the tradition of the Druids has been perceived as Pythagorean by observers since ancient times. Diodorus of Sicily held that the Druids followed the Pythagorean doctrine, in particular regarding the fate of the soul, and so it is of interest that the axis we have been considering throughout the European landscape aligns with this doctrine. The evidence in the Welsh language is certainly revealing, with the word *pythagori* meaning "to explain the system of the universe."[8] The persistence of this view no doubt accounts for the efforts of John Wood the Elder in the 18th century to identify the legendary King Bladud, who discovered the healing springs at Bath and constructed wings to fly, with Abaris the Hyperborean, the follower of Apollo and companion of Pythagoras who flew by means of his golden arrow.

---

[7] This evaluation is echoed by John Michell in his comment regarding other landmarks on the alignment he discovered: "If the Cheesewring and the Burrowbridge Mump are indeed artificial, they must be far older than the works of the megalith builders and form part of an earlier, more gigantic system of geomancy" (Michell and Rhone 1991, pages 135-6).

[8] William Owen, *A Dictionary of the Welsh Language*, London, 1803.

This association of Pythagoras with the tradition of the Celts may be compared with certain indications presented in *The Red and the White*. Above all, it should be recalled that according to René Guénon, the name of the Celts and Chaldeans is the same, and designates not a particular people, but rather a shared sacerdotal authority.[9] According to Classical sources, the Chaldeans were among the teachers of Pythagoras during his travels; and in the description of the three forms of Hermes according to Abu Ma`shar al-Balkhi, Pythagoras is singled out as belonging to the school of Hermes' second form who is the source of Chaldean authority.[10] More specifically, Porphyry relates that the Chaldeans taught Pythagoras astronomy, and this in turn should be compared with the memory of the Druids' "Three Sublime Astronomers." They are named as Don, who is

---

[9] Page 22.

[10] Page 29. Given the importance of the site known as Göbekli Tepe in understanding the Chaldean tradition, it is worth noting that evidence has recently been presented that an equilateral triangle is formed by the centers of its three main enclosures (Gil Haklay and Avi Gopher, "Geometry and Architectural Planning at Göbekli Tepe, Turkey," *Cambridge Archaeological Journal*, volume 20, issue 2, Cambridge: Cambridge University Press, May 2020, pages 343-57). The observation that human features are only adorning the megaliths of the northern enclosure suggest the site's integrated plan, as well as its relationship to the Hyperborean source. Most remarkably, however, recent research reveals a change of direction at the site, with the oldest enclosures being oriented to the north whereas later ones appear oriented to the east-west axis (Andrew Collins, *The Cygnus Key*, Rochester: Bear & Company, 2018, pages 26-7). This demonstrates the developments outlined above on page 26 perfectly, and deserves a fuller treatment; but it should at least be noted that the presence of panthers upon the stones of the later enclosure known as the "Lion Pillars Building" makes René Guénon's comments on Nimrod in his article "Seth" (Guénon 2004) all the more essential in evaluating the significance of this change in direction (cf. *The Red and the White*, page 31).

the father of Arianrhod and many others, Gwyn Ap Nudd, who as King of the Fairies is said to reside within Glastonbury Tor and lead the Wild Hunt,[11] and Idris, a mythological figure whose Welsh name is, very remarkably, the Arabic name of the antediluvian Hermes. Just as this first Hermes may be understood as the Hyperborean progenitor of the second Hermes' Chaldean authority, we find here in the recurrence of the name Idris confirmation that whatever their traditions were, the Celts and Chaldeans represent a singular wisdom.

There is a mountain in Wales with the name Cader Idris, literally the "Seat of Idris," where that astronomer is said to have watched the skies. This Idris is also characterized as being giant in stature, a not uncommon attribute of antediluvian humanity. However, evil giants likewise figure in the lore of Britain's foundation, and given the course of the Saint Michael Line, it is worth recalling that legends place the last stronghold of these giants in Cornwall.[12] King Arthur himself is held to have fought a giant at Saint Michael's Mount.[13] For Guénon, such legends of giants are to be traced to the Nimrodian opposition to Chaldean sacerdotal authority, and this context is particularly relevant here.[14] In any case, the matter of giants provides another example of the dual nature of symbols, alternatively luminous and dark; and

---

[11] Cf. chapter 4 of *The Red and the White* on the Hyperborean representatives known in Ireland as the Tuatha dé Danann who became identified with the fairies in their subterranean realm.

[12] According to Geoffrey of Monmouth, Albion had been named after the giant of that name, but the Trojan commander Brutus renamed the land Britain after himself; the defeat of the giant Goemagot by the Trojan warrior Corineus results in Cornwall being named for him. Even so, a comparison between the name Cornwall and the name of Apollo Karneios would not be out of place here, especially given the Celtic etymology of the former.

[13] Even Demir Baba of the Balkans killed an evil giant for the Czar of Russia (Hasluck, op. cit., page 296).

[14] *The Red and the White*, page 31.

given the recent popular interest in "ancient giants," it is essential to heed Guénon's warning that "the confusion between the luminous and dark aspects is what properly constitutes 'satanism.'"[15]

Given the presence of Idris in this triad of Druidic authorities, we should further consider the triad of Islamic esoterism that is formed by the Qutb and his two assistants or Imams.[16] Just as Idris as the Qutb is regarded as ever-living, so too are the Imams associated with the living prophets Elijah and Jesus. Concerning Jesus, of course, there is no more important location in Britain to acknowledge than Glastonbury upon the Saint Michael Line. In his works, John Michell has highlighted and interpreted the wealth of evidence for Glastonbury being the first and most distinguished Christian site in Britain, if not the world. The traditional understanding is that Saint Joseph of Arimathea personally founded the first settlement there, and there is a reminder of this in the Glastonbury Thorn tree that according to legend miraculously grew from the saint's staff. With this Joseph being the uncle of Jesus, local stories have imagined Jesus as a boy reaching Glastonbury from Cornwall alongside his uncle. This notion persists above all in the British hymn and national anthem "Jerusalem," the musical adaptation of the poem "And Did Those Feet in Ancient Time" by William Blake. Near the end of Cornwall in St.

---

[15] Guénon 2001, page 19. While the giant Idris may represent the primordial and so Hyperborean tradition, the evil giants might easily be associated with remnants of the Atlantean tradition that was destroyed by the Flood. Even so, the name Albion indicates a legitimate origin, and Guénon specifically cites "Albion and Albania" as examples of designations of spiritual centers (page 65).

[16] In "The Land of the Sun," Guénon draws attention to "three points of the triangle" that Maltwood posits at the center of the Glastonbury Zodiac in Butleigh, and this should be considered in light of his reference elsewhere to a triangular signature of the Pole.

Just, there is a holy well with a footprint in stone, and this footprint is attributed to Jesus.[17]

During the Middle Ages, the graves of Christian saints were the focus of veneration at the great Abbey; in fact, Saint Patrick himself was understood to be buried there, having served as the Abbot of Glastonbury. As patron saint of Ireland, his importance for the Celts is clear enough, and this in turn demonstrates the importance of Glastonbury. However, Ireland claims another tomb for Saint Patrick, at Down Cathedral in Downpatrick in Northern Ireland. Now, rather than casting doubt on the veracity of either claim, or of positing the existence of two Saint Patricks, this unusual example in Christendom might instead be compared with the phenomenon of certain Muslim saints having multiple tombs. We have already considered the specific case of Sari Saltik, and other examples may doubtless be found.[18]

It is, however, an Irish saint reputedly buried alongside Saint Patrick who especially concerns us here, the martyr Saint Indracht, although his significance to the Saint Michael Line has been overlooked until now. It was mentioned before that this alignment appears to correspond to sunrise on the cross-quarter day in May, yet careful calculation indicates that the sunrise of 1 May is rather too early. The feast day of Saint Indracht is 8 May, and is, in fact, the very day that the landscape alignment corresponds to the orientation with the sunrise. That 8 May is also the festival of the Apparition

---

[17] Janet Bord, *Footprints in Stone*, Loughborough: Heart of Albion Press, 2004, page 41.

[18] `Ali bin Abi Talib, the Shah-i Mardan, has no less than seven tombs in Central Asia. Evliya Çelebi muses on the multiple tombs of his spiritual patron Sa`d bin Abi Waqqas, the "Chevalier of Islam" (*faris ul-Islam*) and one of the ten most distinguished Companions of the Prophet, although even he appears to have been unaware of another tomb for the saint in China.

of Saint Michael at Gargano confirms at the very least the connection between the British alignment and the axis through Europe. That is not all: according to the 12th century *Passio sancti Indracti*, a column of light reveals the site of Saint Indracht's martyrdom on his feast day.[19] Curiously, a discrepancy has been found between the most likely date of the saint's martyrdom in March and this festival in May, and so we are left with the likelihood that authorities in Glastonbury were well aware of how this date specifically held the secret of a luminous line upon the landscape.

The effective knowledge of such things did not survive the Reformation. The "suppression" of the Abbey suppressed the sanctity of the site. John Michell insists that the monks, as well as the Druids before them, had practiced sacred chant in "perpetual choirs" by which the land was made harmonious in the Pythagorean sense,[20] and that the loss of this practice brought nothing less than the "disenchantment" of Britain. Still, he offers a valuable hope from a tradition that had been preserved in the Abbey library, that the tomb of Saint Patrick, and so also presumably of Saint Indracht, would one day be rediscovered;[21] and this hope, no doubt, is bound up with another of Michell's revelations, that local lore maintains that one day Jesus will walk again from Cornwall to Glastonbury, and that villagers must be prepared for this.[22] For now, the sanctity of the site is at the very least

---

[19] On Saint Indracht, see Michael Lapidge, "The Cult of St Indracht at Glastonbury," *Anglo-Latin Literature, 900-1066*, London: The Hambledon Press, 1993. According to the *Passio*, Saint Indracht had nine companions; if details in this account were invented, as Lapidge suspects, there is an indication here of Pythagoreanism, since the Pythagoreans swore by the number ten in the triangular form of the tetractys.

[20] Michell and Rhone 1991, page 70.

[21] Michell 1983, page 169.

[22] Michell and Rhone 1991, page 137.

preserved in the descendants of the Glastonbury Thorn,[23] and every year a flowering branch of the holy tree is sent to adorn the British sovereign's table at the feast of Christmas, for it is a sign of this sanctity that the thorn blooms twice a year, at the seasons of both solstices.

More obscure is the claim that the Holy Grail itself, having been brought by its guardian Saint Joseph of Arimathea, is yet hidden in the waters of Glastonbury's most revered spring, the Chalice Well. René Guénon mentions Glastonbury's claims to the Grail in "The Land of the Sun," and explains elsewhere that possession of the Grail represents the "integral preservation of the Primordial Tradition" in a spiritual center.[24] The supposed immersion of the Grail within Chalice Well may therefore indicate a deeper meaning, since, as we have already discovered, the presence of a sacred spring may itself be considered a sign of the Primordial Tradition. With this in mind, it is worth acknowledging that the monumental "pyramids" that formerly towered above the Abbey burials were in actuality triangular "cairns," and Guénon relates this Celtic word to the formulation of Apollo Karneios.[25] Still in keeping with this Hyperborean current, a special stone discovered a little more than a century ago on the Abbey grounds, one of the so-called "Egg Stones," was recognized as an

---

[23] The survival of the sacred thorn's descendants is not only in spite of the Reformation, but also despite recurring monstrous acts of vandalism in very recent years.

[24] Guénon 2001, page 29. John Michell came to accept Guénon's authority on Grail symbolism wholeheartedly (cf. Michell and Rhone 1991, page 9). It is worth noting that Guénon draws attention to a particular story of the Grail's origin that concerns Saint Michael, according to which it had been fashioned by angels from a stone that dropped from Lucifer's forehead during his fall.

[25] See "The Symbolism of Horns." According to William of Malmesbury, these cairns were at least 26 and 18 feet high respectively.

omphalos, and so explicitly related to the temple at Delphi;[26] however, it has not generally been recognized that the depression on its surface may very well be a footprint.

Be that as it may, Medieval literature concerning the Matter of Britain consistently reported the eventual return of the Grail to the East. Given the ascendancy of Islam in that direction, this return is but another facet of the role of Islam in the Grail legends, a subject that has thankfully been examined by Pierre Ponsoye in *L'Islam et le Graal*. On this matter, the words of Guénon's successor, Michel Vâlsan, should suffice here: "the fact that, apropos the two traditional lines of its origin, respectively Celtic and Christian, one could observe from the start certain positive interventions on the part of Islamic esoterism that only confirms its axial and ultimately integrating role, played in a general fashion in Islam and more rarely as regards the traditional West."[27]

A very recent intervention of Islamic esoterism at Glastonbury has been examined in a study called "From Celts to Kaaba" by Ian K.B. Draper.[28] This work focuses on the presence of Naqshbandi Sufis in the town, and since the author mentions their dancing after the example of Mevlana Rumi, there is here a curious echo of the Pythagorean music and dance alluded to above. Draper considers this practice "somewhat controversial," but it is rooted in the personality of the master of the order, Shaykh Nazim `Adil al-Haqqani of Cyprus, a descendant of Rumi who visited Glastonbury in 1999. Although the spiritual guide had been visiting England for very many years in order to meet the needs of Westerners, he had

---

[26] Cf. Frederick Bligh Bond, "The 'Egg Stone' at Glastonbury Abbey," *Proceedings of the Somersetshire Archæological & Natural History Society*, volume 59, 1914.

[27] *L'Islam et la Fonction de René Guénon*, Paris: Editions de l'Œuvre, 1984, page 43.

[28] This appears as chapter 8 in *Sufism in Europe and North America* (Abingdon: Routledge, 2004).

apparently never visited Glastonbury before, and 1999 would mark the end of his annual visits to England. Shaykh Nazim al-Haqqani was the 40th master in the so-called Golden Chain of the Naqshbandi Order, a line of spiritual descent of which the Bektashi Order has traditionally been considered a branch, and his place in that line might easily be understood as having manifested a fullness that is qualitatively signified by the number 40. Perhaps the whirling of his dervishes likewise served to express this fullness. During his visit, Shaykh Nazim said in a talk open to the public, "I am saying to you about Jesus Christ that he was traveling from East to West from North to South;" privately, he clarified the matter of Jesus in Glastonbury, revealing that he had indeed been physically present in the place by means of his spiritual power.

In the teachings of the Greatest Master of Islamic esoterism, Jesus Christ has been called the Alchemist, and in the language of Alchemy, physical matter may be transformed into its most perfect form through the Philosopher's Stone. Doctor John Dee reportedly obtained a small quantity of a red substance identified as the Philosopher's Stone, and of all places it had been discovered in the ruins of Glastonbury Abbey.[29] As he stood in front of the Abbey in 1999, the spiritual master known to his followers as the Red Sulphur among saints said: "This is the spiritual heart of England. Now I understand why Grandsheikh (Sheikh Abdullah Daghistani, Sheikh Nazim's Sheikh) has been sending me to this island for all these years. It is from here that the spiritual new age will begin and to here that Jesus will return."[30]

---

[29] Benjamin Woolley, *The Queen's Conjurer*, New York: Henry Holt and Company, 2001, page 169.
[30] https://www.healing-hearts.co.uk/glastonbury.htm, retrieved January 2021.

Sultan al-Awliya' Shaykh Nazim `Adil al-Haqqani in Britain, 1991

8

The Balance of Britain

Previous considerations of the Axis of Saint Michael and of Apollo have failed to respect its solsticial orientation. The evidence presented earlier concerning the harmonic positions of significant sites upon the axis has only confirmed the importance of this orientation, since both represent aspects of the Pythagorean legacy. The relevance of the Sun's position is indisputable in the Eastern Mediterranean where the alignment was discovered by Jean Richer; however, while the extension of the line by Lucien Richer was an essential contribution, certain particulars of this extension have eclipsed solsticial considerations in favor of connecting dots on a map. This is particularly evident in the example of Skellig Michael, an island off the coast of Ireland with well-preserved ruins of a Christian hermitage upon its rocky heights.[1] While Mont Saint-Michel may be understood to be very near indeed to the corridor that proceeds in the direction of the summer solstice sunset from Mount Carmel, it is very clear that this solstice sunset does not by any stretch of the imagination lead from Mont Saint-Michel to Skellig Michael. However, if we expand the

---

[1] This hermitage relates to the so-called Culdee movement (Walter Horn et al., *The Forgotten Hermitage of Skellig Michael*, Berkeley: University of Press, 1990, page 76); and while the name "Culdee" is supposed to derive from the Gaelic "Célí Dé" ("Companions of God"), its similarity to "Celt" and "Chaldean" is indeed remarkable.

The Balance of Britain

1. Mont Saint-Michel
2. Saint Michael's Mount
3. Skellig Michael
4. Burrowbridge Mump
5. Glastonbury
6. Ogbourne Saint George

Figure 6
British alignments according to the solar azimuths of 8 May

significance of 8 May on the liturgical calendar that was formerly observed at Glastonbury and at Mount Gargano, we discover that the setting Sun on 8 May leads very accurately from Mont Saint-Michel to Skellig Michael via a trajectory near to Saint Michael's Mount in Cornwall. West Penwith is thus remarkably equipoised between sunrise and sunset alignments on 8 May, as may be observed in figure 6. Among other things, this establishes beyond doubt that the direction should be understood as proceeding from Mont Saint-Michel and not the other way round, since sunrise on a day in mid-November or early February, when the alignment would lead from Britain to Normandy, has no apparent relevance to our subject.

Despite all this, every study of the axis has somewhat uncritically begun from the west, ignoring the absence of a solsticial trajectory from Skellig Michael. The proper solar corridor might more naturally be associated with the Channel Islands of Guernsey and Jersey, especially since their positions seem to match somewhat its trajectory. Despite these islands having nothing whatsoever to do with possible alignments from Skellig Michael, the dowsers Broadhurst and Miller explored them anyway, and in fact found the energy they were seeking. They overlooked, unfortunately, the presence of footprints in stone attributed to the Virgin Mary there.[2] Continuing beyond Mount Carmel at the end of their journey, Broadhurst and Miller arrive, significantly enough, at a place associated with Armageddon, and so reflect upon the end of a world. Keeping in mind the relationship of macrocosm to microcosm, however, it may be offered that the end of the physical world suggests rather the beginning of a journey for the soul, which is precisely what an alignment to the summer

---

[2] Bord, op. cit., page 76. This attribution may therefore be considered alongside the other references to the presence of Jesus in Britain.

solstice would indicate for the Pythagoreans. Looking east, even though they declare that "now is the time of the great re-awakening,"[3] the dowsers conclude their investigations rather unfortunately at a ruined temple of Baal, the one whose worship the prophet Elijah historically opposed.[4] Not only is Elijah the legitimate spiritual authority positioned at Mount Carmel, a reality accepted by all three Abrahamic traditions, but given the comment of Shaykh Nazim al-Haqqani, the "new age" should rather be associated with the other end of the solar axis. Indeed, it is the British Isles that must be recognized as having a special relationship with the cross-quarter day of spring, when the earth enjoys its annual "re-awakening."

Before his passing in 2014,[5] Shaykh Nazim `Adil al-Haqqani would have occasion to return to the subject of Glastonbury, this time in the context of the sacred landscape of Britain as a whole. He spoke in 2011 of the "Seven Spiritual Centers" of Britain, although he only specified five of them: "I like Glastonbury. There is spirituality there and in Nelson[6] there is also spirituality,

---

[3] Op. cit., page 368.

[4] The name "Baal" and the Celtic name of the "shining" Apollo seem similar, but their etymology is separate and they should not be confused. Still, this similarity may be understood as that of a shadow to its source, as we have considered in relation to the spirit of Metatron.

[5] In "From Celts to Kaaba," the author mentions rags tied to trees on Glastonbury Tor, and muses that this is "a global phenomenon practiced also at some Sufi sites: for example at the shrine of a Bulgarian Bektashi sheikh in the Rhondope Mountains." Since this Bulgarian shrine must in fact be that of Otman Baba, there is a coincidence here between this Abdal and Shaykh Nazim: both passed away on the 8th of Rajab, the 7th month of the lunar Hijri calendar.

[6] Curiously, it has been claimed that the area of Nelson holds a landscape zodiac akin to that of Glastonbury, the "Pendle Zodiac." Pendle Hill is also the place where the founder of the Quaker movement experienced his vision of a saintly assembly.

as well as Windsor,[7] Edinburgh,[8] and the last point of Scotland."[9] He further provided an indication of the composition of these centers by identifying Edinburgh as the "Moonlight Center." Now, the Moon belongs, of course, to the seven planets of traditional cosmology, and we have already referred to the ordering of the Earth into seven climates. Significantly, both septads are placed in precise correspondence with the saintly rank of the Abdal by the Greatest Master of Islamic esoterism, Muhyiddin Ibn ʿArabi:

> The Abdal are seven, never more nor less. Through them Allah watches over the seven terrestrial climates. In each climate there is a Badal who governs it. The first among them represents (literally "is on the foot of") the Friend of God (Abraham) and occupies the first climate; the second represents the Divine Interlocutor (Moses), the third represents Aaron, the fourth Idris, the fifth Joseph, the sixth Jesus, the seventh Adam. They possess the knowledge of the planets.[10]

There is no reason to exclude the possibility of a secondary localization of this same principle in the

---

[7] In *The Merry Wives of Windsor,* Shakespeare locates the ghostly Herne the Hunter there, and so we find in Windsor a formulation of the Wild Hunt.

[8] Edinburgh is called the "Athens of the North." Like Rome, the city was founded on seven hills.

[9] https://sufilive.com/Advice-to-Mureeds-in-England-3328-EN-print.html, retrieved January 2021.

[10] *La Parure des Abdâl*, translated and annotated by Michel Vâlsan, Milano: Archè, 2018, page 40. Just as the Abdal are assigned the planetary spheres, so too are they assigned authority over the days of the week, providing a clearer formulation of the system described in the opening chapter that is everywhere followed despite its confused attachment to Norse and Roman pantheons.

cosmos of Britain;[11] after all, besides the close association of Jesus with Glastonbury, we have already discovered a "seat" of Idris in Wales.[12] Cader Idris has an additional characteristic to recommend it as an unrecognized center, that when considered on the map of Britain, it appears spatially compatible with the positions of the other specified centers. Also, while the expression "last point of Scotland" is not too precise, there happens to be a place in the Shetland Islands that involves a coincidence of names akin to the example of Idris: the place name of Mousa, with its unusually well-preserved broch or circular stone fort, is a homophone of Musa, the Arabic name of Moses, who is specifically named above. Alternatively, the "last point of Scotland" might refer to a point closer to the end of the mainland, such as the Orkneys, which would still not rule out the candidacy of Mousa. In any case, when all of the above-mentioned places are plotted on a map as in figure 7, the seven points form an inevitably recognizable asterism.[13] This arrangement of sites is obviously distinct from the matter of alignments, but the latter relates to the psychic domain especially, while this arrangement relates primarily to the spiritual domain. Even so, the two domains may be understood to converge on the point of Glastonbury. For

---

[11] It is conceivable that the localization of this principle in other lands would give rise to connections between them, and this in turn might help explain why British Israelism insists on Edinburgh being the actual location of Jerusalem, Glastonbury the location of Bethel, etc.

[12] There are, in fact, footprints in stone upon Cader Idris as well as Pendle Hill, though in both cases, apparently, they are attributed to the Devil (Bord, op. cit., pages 113 and 115).

[13] Like the seven tombs of Sari Saltik, these centers may be contrasted with the "Seven Towers of the Devil" mentioned by René Guénon (*Insights into Islamic Esoterism and Taoism*, Hillsdale: Sophia Perennis, 2003, page 68), especially since he considers the latter to be the counterfeit of a reality pertaining to the seven "terrestrial 'Poles,'" by which he means the Abdal.

Paths of the Sun

1	Glastonbury
2	Nelson
3	Windsor
4	Edinburgh
5	Mousa (projected)
6	Cader Idris (projected)
7	"Last point of Scotland" (approximate)

Figure 7
The Seven Spiritual Centers and the Scales of Britain

that matter, perhaps it should be insisted that Glastonbury also embodies a remarkable point of convergence between the writings of René Guénon and the teachings of Shaykh Nazim al-Haqqani.

Regarding the asterism suggested by the Seven Spiritual Centers, the configuration of the land naturally supports this pattern. Due to the position of the islands beyond Scotland, the asterism seems to belong to Ursa Minor rather than the more familiar Ursa Major (unless the "last point in Scotland" refers to a place in the Outer Hebrides). Of course, with the Pole Star belonging to Ursa Minor, this may very well be an important distinction, but if we return to "The Land of the Sun" by Guénon, we find that this distinction really needn't concern us. It is perhaps more essential to recognize that the significance of both constellations here was anticipated by the author in that article, despite them not being part of the zodiac:

> …it is important to note that the Zodiac of Glastonbury presents some peculiarities which from our point of view can be regarded as marks of its "authenticity;" and indeed, to begin with it seems that the sign of the Scales (Libra) is missing. Now, as we have explained elsewhere, the celestial Scales were not always zodiacal, but were at first polar, the name having been applied originally to the Great Bear, or to the Great Bear and Little Bear taken together (and by a remarkable coincidence the name of Arthur is directly linked to the symbolism of these constellations).[14]

The relevance of the Scales to our subject should be immediately apparent. They are the emblem of the

---

[14] Op. cit., page 91. Ursa Major is traditionally known also as Arthur's Wain. Ursa Minor is nearest to the constellation Draco, just as Arthur is the son of Pendragon, providing an example of the beneficent aspect of the symbolism of the dragon.

celestial Pole Saint Michael, whose name is attached as a rule to the high places along these alignments, especially along the alignment to Glastonbury. Suggesting an awareness of the symbolism under consideration, Gildas in the 6th century relates a tradition that describes Britain as being "poised in the divine balance, as it is said, which supports the whole world."[15]

The symbolism of the scales, or *mizan* in Arabic,[16] is particularly important to the teachings of Islamic esoterism, and the word appears repeatedly in the Holy Qur'an. The alchemist Jabir bin Hayyan makes particular mention of Pythagoras in his elucidation of the doctrine of the Mizan, rendered in English as the "Balance," according to which all things are knowable through a weighing of the hidden and manifest aspects encoded in their names. In his unparalleled study of the principles of sacred geography, *The King of the World*, René Guénon considers a particular name with an Arabic and Hebrew root in the context of the scales: "*Haq* is the power that establishes the rule of Justice, that is, the equilibrium symbolized by the scales, whereas power itself is symbolized by the sword, which is exactly what characterizes the essential role of the royal power; in the spiritual order, on the other hand, it is the power of Truth."[17] Obviously, it is important to observe that this

---

[15] *De Excidio Britonum*.

[16] It will be observed that the word *mizan* mirrors the name Nazim, which is remarkable enough on its own, but this is only true in English, since the English letter z stands in this case for two different Arabic letters. Still, it is also true that his family name `Adil signifies "the Just."

[17] Guénon 2001, page 38. Guénon draws attention to the numerical value of the word *haq* in gematria, 108, as well as the relevance of this number in Hinduism, so it is worth adding that the same value belongs to the word *mizan* (40 + 10 + 7 + 1 + 50 = 108). For his part, John Michell emphasizes the importance of this number in *The New View Over Atlantis* (op. cit., pages 155-6).

same word is the root of the title "Haqqani" of the master who revealed the existence of the Seven Spiritual Centers. This title has furthermore been applied to the order itself, and so it is now more properly known as the Naqshbandi-Haqqani Order. In the context of the polar significance of this title, it is worth recognizing that Shaykh Nazim had two principal assistants in his work, Shaykh Adnan Kabbani and Shaykh Hisham Kabbani, who, as brothers, so obviously served as the closest conceivable formulation of the twin Imams under the Qutb. Even more explicitly linked to the scales, the name Kabbani is from the Arabic word *qabban* that names a particular variation of the scales, but one that still belongs fully to this symbolism.

Based on the primordial identification of the Scales with the constellation of Ursa Major, Guénon further explains that the Sanskrit name of the Scales, Tula, often appears in the naming of sacred centers.[18] According to the Hindu doctrines, there is an important correspondence between this constellation and the Seven Rishis who preserve wisdoms from a former age, though Guénon insists that this correspondence was shifted to the Pleiades when the Scales became part of the zodiac.[19] These shifts away from Hyperborean formulations correspond in Greek cosmology to the loss of the Golden Age of Kronos. Very remarkably, Plutarch writes of a British tradition regarding an island "in the direction of the summer sunset," where "Kronos himself sleeps confined in a deep cave of rock that shines like gold...and birds flying in over the summit of the rock bring ambrosia to him, and all the island is suffused with fragrance scattered from the rock as from a fountain; and those spirits mentioned before tend and serve Kronos, having

---

[18] The idea of "Thule" in relation to Britain was introduced by the Greek explorer Pytheas of Massalia, whose name is of interest in the Pythagorean context, and whose characterization of Britain as a triangle is therefore of particular significance.
[19] Guénon, 2001, chapter 10.

been his comrades what time he ruled as king over gods and men."[20] By the Middle Ages, this British tradition had been supplanted by accounts of the continued existence of King Arthur and his knights. In addition to the places already mentioned, the supernatural survival of King Arthur has been linked to several locations upon the Saint Michael Line in Britain, including Saint Michael's Mount in Cornwall and "a cave under a hill near Glastonbury," where he is moreover named as a leader of the Wild Hunt.[21] In fact, "belief in Arthur's continued life was sufficiently powerful in 1113 to almost cause a riot in Cornwall when it was contradicted by sceptical French canons."

In Islamic terms, a comparable preservation of ancient sanctity is exemplified in the *Yiti Kalandar*, the Companions of the Cave, who sheltered for centuries under the earth during an age of tyranny. In his commentary on the Qur'anic Chapter of the Cave in which their story appears, al-Qashani provides the following description: "Know that the Companions of the Cave are the seven saints charged with preserving the Divine Order in the world: it only subsists through them. They remain at all times according to the number and the hierarchy of the planets." The identification of the Companions of the Cave with the Abdal should be sufficiently clear.[22] Louis Massignon, in his elucidation of the importance of the Seven Sleepers in Christianity and

---

[20] Moralia 12.
[21] Thomas Green, "'But Arthur's Grave is Nowhere Seen:' Twelfth-Century and Later Solutions to Arthur's Current Whereabouts," *Arthuriana: Early Arthurian Tradition and the Origin of the Legend*, Louth: The Lindes Press, 2009, page 246. The author explains that the Medieval discovery of Arthur's grave in Glastonbury Abbey was a fraud perpetrated against people's faith in his return.
[22] A seven-fold spiritual authority was likewise recognized in ancient Mesopotamian religion; by a strange linguistic coincidence they were known in Sumerian as Abgal.

Islam, provides further evidence of these seven saints being identified with the rank of the Abdal.[23] What must be emphasized is the correspondence between the celestial order and what is hidden in the earth, "since whatever is at the lowest level corresponds, by inverse analogy, to what is at the highest level."[24] We have already observed examples of this correspondence in the Glastonbury Zodiac, as well as in the persistent indication of sanctity specifically through footprints. The legend of Emperor Frederick II yet living within the earth may also be recalled here, especially since his mediation between the worlds of Christendom and Islam echoes the shared veneration of the Seven Sleepers.

In Christianity and Islam alike, the Sleepers must awaken and emerge from concealment. Above all, then, the revelation of the Seven Centers as embodiments of the presence of the Abdal in the landscape should in itself be recognized as a stage in the uncovering of a once hidden reality. In the context of the Matter of Britain, this reality belongs to King Arthur and his knights, especially as the embodiment of the "royal power" that along with spiritual power is indicated by the word *Haq*. As for the Haqqani spiritual master who revealed the existence of these Centers in a Christian land, we may recall the note by Michel Vâlsan: "…in Islamic esoterism, and according to its proper 'perspective,' it is said that the Qutb provides his providential help not only to Muslims, but also to the Christians and Jews, and that this perhaps relates, in any case, to the general role of the Islamic tradition as intermediary between East and West in the last part of the traditional cycle, although it is…the most recent of the current traditional forms, because of which it is assured

---

[23] See the relevant articles in *Opera Minora*, volume 3, Liban: Dar al-Maaref, 1963. Massignon specifies the festival of the Companions of the Cave to be 18 Rajab.
[24] René Guénon, *The Reign of Quantity and the Signs of the Times*, Baltimore: Penguin Books, 1972, page 186.

of a greater vitality compared to more ancient traditions."[25]

---

[25] "Les derniers hautes grades de l'Écossisme et la réalisation descendante," *Études Traditionnelles*, Paris, 1953.

9

Renewal

In "The Land of the Sun," René Guénon makes a significant observation regarding the Glastonbury Zodiac: "the whole complex calls to mind the works of the ancient mound builders of North America." Now in the following century, academia is beginning to uncover the truth of this statement. There is a growing acknowledgement, starting with the proposition of George E. Lankford, that the most distinguished of the North American mounds, the so-called Great Serpent Mound, is a representation of the constellation Scorpio. The comparison with the stellar effigies of Glastonbury would now appear to be especially relevant. More significantly, the archaeologist William F. Romain in "Adena-Hopewell Earthworks and the Milky Way Path of Souls"[1] presents a convincing case that these mound builders oriented their works in relation to celestial azimuths, including those of the solstices, in arrangements throughout landscapes much larger than earlier supposed. Examining the linear path known as the Great Hopewell Road with its length of some 60 miles, the author explains that its design mirrors the Milky Way as a pathway for souls. Such a path upon the landscape

---

[1] *Tracing the Relational: The Archaeology of Worlds, Spirits, and Temporalities*, edited by Buchanan and Skousen, Salt Lake City: University of Utah Press, 2015, pages 54-82.

should, of course, be identified as a ley line,[2] if ley lines weren't categorically rejected by modern science. More importantly, if the description by Porphyry regarding the purpose of the Pythagorean solsticial paths is recalled, it must then be admitted that the American Indian understanding of the Milky Way is in perfect agreement with that of the Pythagoreans, providing, no doubt, yet another indication of the Primordial Tradition.

This agreement of Pythagorean and American Indian doctrines has been included though not properly admitted in an article by astronomer E.C. Krupp, in which the author provides a survey of traditional understandings of the Milky Way.[3] On the authority of the Mithraic scholar Franz Cumont, he relates that in Classical Antiquity the Milky Way was originally regarded as the path of the Sun. He also cites other examples from the American Indian tradition, such as an account from the Ajumawi or Pit River Indians of California. The Ajumawi live southeast of the volcanic Mount Shasta, the traditional World Axis of the region,[4] and so the azimuth of sunset on the summer solstice for them leads towards the mountain; and indeed, "the Ajumawi say the Milky Way is aligned at this time when the trail followed on the earth by the dead and aligned with the Sun as well."

---

[2] Similarly, other structures in North America might be profitably compared with the "tor enclosures" of Britain; perhaps not without reason, these same structures were often attributed historically to the Welsh Prince Madoc (cf. *The Red and the White*, chapter 1).

[3] E.C. Krupp, "Negotiating the Highwire of Heaven: The Milky Way and the Itinerary of the Soul," *Vistas in Astronomy*, volume 39, issue 4, 1995.

[4] It may not be entirely fanciful that Glastonbury and Mount Shasta are consistently imagined to be two of seven "world chakras," a notion that may be traced to Crowley's inheritor Kenneth Grant in *The Magical Revival*.

The neighboring Modocs traditionally lived northeast of this mountain, and Modoc legends explicitly mention the path or road of the Sun that also relates to the fate of the soul.[5] The creator Gmukamps (Kumush) "had the power to revive people from the dead by retrieving their souls from this path."[6] The sacred geography of the Modoc is centered on Tule Lake, although the name recorded by Jeremiah Curtin is rather Tula Lake, and Tula, as we have seen, is among the traditional names for a sacred center. Given that this landscape includes a solsticial alignment with Mount Shasta, it is of interest that certain volcanic buttes along this alignment are traditionally included among the "stair steps" of the Creator. Moreover, this understanding may be compared with that of the Ajumawi:

> Pit River oral tradition likewise depicts alignments of buttes on both the north and south sides of the Highlands as being the "footprints" or "stopping over" points of the Creator. Many (if not all) of these cinder cone buttes were formerly used for religious purposes, and some are still used for these purposes today.[7]

This last statement may be true for the Ajumawi, but the bloody campaigns of the Indian War north of the Highlands ended with the final removal of the Modoc

---

[5] See for example "Kumush and His Daughter" In Jeremiah Curtin, *Myths of the Modocs*, Boston: Little, Brown, and Company, 1912.
[6] Don Hamm and Gordon Bettles, "House of the Rising Sun," *Talking With the Past: The Ethnography of Rock Art*, edited by Keyser et al., Portland: Oregon Archaeological Society, 2006, page 183.
[7] Douglas Deur, *In the Footprints of Gmukamps*, Pacific West Region: National Park Service, 2008, page 190.

from the lands of Tule Lake.[8] Like the last Abbot of Glastonbury, the leaders of the Modoc were hung for maintaining the traditions of a sacred land. Tule Lake was drained; but attached to one of its surrounding buttes that is said to be "Gmukamps Bed" is a legend that recalls nothing more than those of the sleeping King Arthur:

> Someday Kamookumputs will surely wake up and look out over the world he made. He may be angry at how things have changed and bring the water back to cover Tule Lake again, changing the world to be like it was when he first made it.[9]

Clearly, the matter of solar paths and the themes relating to them should not be understood as belonging only to the European milieu[10].

There is a distinction to be observed between the Modoc and Ajumawi examples of paths for souls and the physically cleared route of the Great Hopewell Road. Along with the latter may be mentioned the so-called Chaco Roads that run over great distances in the American southwest, that may or may not have an apparent relationship to celestial azimuths. Indeed, the more general folkloric association of straight paths with the psychic realm does not require them to. What

---

[8] On the Modoc War, see Jim Compton, *Spirit in the Rock: The Fierce Battle for Modoc Homelands*, Pullman: Washington State University Press, 2017.

[9] Cited in the pamphlet "Petroglyph Point: An Interpretive Walk" published by Lava Beds National Monument and Lava Beds Natural History Association. Cf. "Where Koomookumpts Sleeps" in Thomas Doty, *Doty Meets Coyote*, Ashland: Blackstone, 2016.

[10] There has been a modern attempt to identify a solar corridor in North America called the "Hammonasset Line," and while its particular importance has literally been overextended, at least researchers have kept in mind solsticial and funerary considerations.

constitutes a path of the Sun is a special distinction among such paths, and as we have seen in these pages, such alignments may have no obvious trace on the ground despite having a physical aspect observable through the abstraction of maps. Nevertheless, regarding the Saint Michael Line in Britain, John Michell imagined that this alignment must have been a pilgrimage route for people, and he extended this interpretation to the Axis of Saint Michael and Apollo.[11] During his life, Michell sought to renew the practice of visiting such sites: "For Michell, encouraging pilgrims to visit Michael sites and tap into their energy will help reduce the chaos of British society and will bring about an enlightened paradise centered at Glastonbury."[12] While a sacred site must be the destination of pilgrims, physical movement along straight alignments between sites is another matter entirely, and the magnitude of the distances covered, the rigors of the terrain, and the absence of roadways all suggest otherwise.

The sacred sites upon the paths of the Sun represent a spiritual sanctification of these straight paths for souls. As we have found in the central example of Mount Gargano, this sanctification may even leave a physical trace, such as a miraculous footprint. We have encountered other examples of this phenomenon; in the world of Islam it is very well known. A site that marks the

---

[11] See Michell's foreword to Broadhurst and Miller, 2000.

[12] Hale, op. cit., 2016, page 188. What Michell envisioned thus anticipated the teaching of Shaykh Nazim al-Haqqani. It might also be admitted that Michell was following the example of Wellesley Tudor Pole, who likewise enjoined a renewal of pilgrimage. The name "Pole" coincidentally reflects the title of the supreme spiritual authority, and it is worth considering the role of the Qutb in the context of Pole's question, "If our Land is destined to contain within itself the New Jerusalem, thereby fulfilling the prophecy of Blake, is it too much to believe that a Holy One from God may already be on its way to our shores from Heavenly realms?" (quoted in ibid., page 186).

passage of a holy one is often called a *qadam-ja*, literally "place of the footprint," even when a footprint is not observed. For example, in Central Asia, a conspicuous basaltic peak is known as `Ali's footstep, and this designation, like with the examples near Mount Shasta, is applied to the entire landmark.[13] More generally, the example of 'Ali, the Shah-i Mardan, who is the supreme spiritual authority in the historical development of Sufism,[14] offers some significant correspondences with the traditions concerning Mount Gargano. To begin with, there are many examples of *qadam-ja* in Central Asia that include visible footprints in stone attributed to `Ali, despite the lack of historical accounts allowing for his presence there. Often enough, the traditions at these sites include reports of dragon slaying, and mention of a wondrous camel; and while a camel is not a bovine, both may be designated as "bulls." Even more remarkably, the memory of `Ali's mysterious passage through Central Asia includes his routine military intervention with the sword Dhul-Fiqar that even appears as a flaming sword.[15] Obviously, all of these elements are present in the account of the foundation of the sanctuary of Saint Michael, and even the end of `Ali's historical record in the 7th century[16] occurs within three years of the battle at which the archangel with the flaming sword appeared atop the

---

[13] Thierry Zarcone, "Shrines (Qadamgāh) and Relics Dedicated to Imam `Ali ibn Abī Tālib in the Turkic and Indo-Persian Areas," *Kyoto Bulletin of Islamic Area Studies*, 13, 2020, page 39.

[14] Recall that the two sons of `Ali with the daughter of the Prophet have nearly identical names, Hasan and Husayn, suggesting an embodiment of the twin Imams at the summit of the spiritual hierarchy.

[15] Irène Mélikoff, *Abū Muslim le "Port-hache" du Khorassan*, Paris: Maisonneuve, 196, page 38.

[16] Sufi orders have preserved the story of `Ali leading the camel that carried his own coffin away from the historical event of his death, and this image frequently appears in Ottoman calligraphic compositions.

mountain. When the site was sanctified, supposedly prior to the battle, it was understood to be consecrated by the archangel himself, and not by a specifically Christian authority; for this reason, the sanctuary at Mount Gargano is known as the "Celestial Basilica," and Saint Francis refused to enter it. No doubt this site is exceptional in Christendom; but in terms of the sacred geography of Islam, it is clearly a *qadam-ja*.

René Guénon was quoted above on the matter of the "substitution" of the name of Saint Michael for that of Apollo, offering that this "changes nothing of the sense;" but if Saint Michael is identified with the transhistorical reality of Metatron, is it not rather Apollo, whose tomb was formerly found at Delphi, who may be said to have served as a substitute for this reality? Indeed, this is how spiritual authority is formulated in Islamic esoterism: while Idris is named as the primordial Qutb with a residence in the solar sphere, this rank is nonetheless embodied on Earth by a succession of Poles.[17] We have already explained that each of the Abdal, who are literally "substitutes," is replaced by another at the end of life, and the Qutb is included among the Abdal. From this perspective, the attribution of the *qadam-ja* at Gargano to the archangel may be correct, but if so, it is more likely that the footprint belongs rather to whomever at that time represented Metatron on Earth, that is, the Qutb, who "provides his providential help not only to Muslims, but also to the Christians." Of course, Roman Christendom would not have shared this perspective for a whole host of reasons, not least because it only recognizes sainthood among the deceased, or as belonging to the angelic realm.

---

[17] At the same time, it must be admitted that in Islamic esoterism, "this structure is itself no more than a refraction of a higher reality whence it derives its authority...`As for the one and only Pole, it is the spirit of Muhammad (*rūh Muhammad*), by which all the Messengers and all the prophets are sustained'" (Chodkiewicz, op. cit., page 94).

Among the Abdal, four are linked to prophets whose historical identities are remembered for having transcended death: Idris, Elijah, Jesus, and al-Khidr (literally the "Green One"). The Hyperborean character of Apollo's principal shrines has a clear link to Idris and the Primordial Tradition, while the sanctuary at Mount Gargano is linked with Metatron and so with Idris. It may further be observed that the two extremities of the solar axis are associated with two others from among these four Awtad. The presence of Jesus is a distinction of Britain at the northwest extension of the alignment, while Mount Carmel and other peaks at the southeast end of the alignment are named for Elijah.[18] It could moreover be insisted that the principle feast of Jesus, Christmas, belongs to the season of the winter solstice, and so at least symbolically to the north, as aforementioned. Less obvious is the connection to be made between the summer solstice and Elijah; yet we have already noted the fixing of the feast of Saint John the Baptist near the summer solstice, and given the naming of John the Baptist as Elijah in the Gospels,[19] we may understand that the presence of Elijah at the southern extension of the solsticial alignment is in perfect balance with the presence of Jesus at the north. The Saint Michael and Apollo Axis, then, might accurately be called an "Axis of the Three Awtad."[20]

---

[18] Given the importance of high places on this alignment, it should be recalled that the function of the Awtad relates specifically to the symbolism of mountains (cf. *The Red and the White*, page 50).

[19] Matthew 11:14. In the Holy Qur'an, there is in fact mention of many Elijahs (XXXVII, 130). For the proper understanding of Jesus and John the Baptist in Islam, see the profoundly important work by Karima Sperling, *The Family of 'Imran: Mary, Jesus, Zachariah, and John* (Little Bird Books, 2020).

[20] In the American Indian mythology of the Modocs, three figures are associated with the "roads of the Sun:" Gmukamps, his brother Was-Gmukamps (whose name suggests but another

As for the fourth of the Awtad, he is by no means absent, since the Green Man is above all associated with the spring and its annual renewal. A Tradition of the Prophet Muhammad reveals that, *"Khidr was so named because he sat on a barren white land once, after which it turned luxuriantly green with vegetation."*[21] Besides the solstices, there has been a date that has consistently figured in our subject, the cross-quarter day that falls about a week into May. Mention was made above of the spring festival on 6 May known as Hidrellez, its association with the Abdal of the Balkans, and its observance by Christians as well as Muslims. In fact, Hidrellez is practically the only example of a holy day on the solar calendar observed by Muslims,[22] whose sacred calendar is based on the Moon. Its name is rooted in the name of the Green Man, and its timing is based on the Christian liturgical calendar, since al-Khidr is known also as Saint George[23] and 6 May is his day. Now, Saint George's Day is reckoned as 23 April according to the Gregorian calendar, but this has corresponded to a day in early May for many centuries according to the Eastern churches that honor the former

---

form of the former), and his son A'isis. Whether or not the similarity between the names of A'isis and Jesus (`Isa in Arabic) is a legacy of European contact, the parallel between these triads of authority over paths of the Sun is no doubt remarkable indeed.

[21] Quoted in Shaykh Muhammad Hisham Kabbani, *The Naqshbandi Sufi Way*, Chicago: Kazi Publications, 1995, page 119. Al-Khidr figures prominently in Islamic esoterism as a teacher of the elite; the source cited here considers his unique role as a link in the spiritual chain of the Naqshbandi-Haqqani Order.

[22] The only comparable example is Saint Elijah's Day on 2 August, known to Balkan Muslims as `Ali Day, when Christians and Muslims go to high places in the landscape to pray for rain. It is worth observing that the Sun's position on this cross-quarter day mirrors its position on the cross-quarter day in May.

[23] This identification of Saint George with al-Khidr may be compared to the identification of the Alexander the Great with Dhul-Qarnayn.

Julian calendar. In a sense, however, the Roman church recognized the importance of this cross-quarter day by fixing a feast of the "solar archangel" on 8 May.[24] The near coincidence of dates between the two calendars is made more unmistakable by the fact that Saint Michael and Saint George are, at least in Christian iconography, both dragon slayers.

Saint George is the patron saint of Genoa upon the solar alignment, as well, of course, of England.[25] On Saint George's Day in England, the hymn "Jerusalem" is more often sung than on any other day, declaring hope in the renewal of Glastonbury. Windsor, another of the Spiritual Centers of Britain, is the location of Saint George's Chapel, headquarters of the most distinguished order of chivalry in the world, the Order of the Garter. Since HRH The Prince of Wales is the Royal Knight Companion of the Garter, it is certainly worth noting that he spoke publicly on the identity of Saint George as al-Khidr.[26] Given that the Saint Michael Line conforms to an orientation with the spring festival, perhaps it should rather be seen as a line belonging to the patron saint of "England's green and pleasant land" instead, and so an "Axis of the Fourth

---

[24] The principal feast of Saint Michael is 29 September, and it should be noted that the feast of 8 May has in modern times been removed from the Catholic calendar.

[25] Among other forms of the Green Man in England, special mention should be made of Robin Hood, not least because his skill with the bow recalls Apollo as well as its importance in Islam. In fact, a recent development of his legend insists on the inclusion of a Muslim in his band, and even his closest companion, Little John, becomes in a most recent example a Muslim named Yahya. This name is, of course, the Arabic name of John the Baptist, who as we have seen is related to Elijah, another of the Awtad. Even more remarkably, the Awtad have assistants according to Islamic esoterism, with the fourth of them being "on the heart" of the prophet Hud, and so the strange name "Hood" is itself relevant to this context.

[26] Speech delivered in tribute at the memorial of King Hussein of Jordan, 5 July 1999.

Awtad." In fact, if the line is extended past Glastonbury and Avebury, as John Michell has indicated, it passes through the center of one place of particular note, "the ancient church at Ogbourne St George, once an important monastic site."[27]

In 2011, the opportunity for Shaykh Nazim al-Haqqani to name five of the Seven Spiritual Centers of Britain arose during a conversation that focused on HRH The Prince of Wales:

> I pray for him to be honored in Eternity, just as he is honored here. I am happy with this book that you brought here (*Harmony*, written by Prince Charles). He has good understanding and is a very clever one. This book is a way of life that people have abandoned and have now fallen in endless troubles, miseries, problems, and crises. If people follow such a way (as mentioned in the book), not going against nature, but are friendly with nature, they will live an excellent and sweet life.[28]

This book *Harmony* is subtitled "A New Way of Looking at Our World," though it would be more accurate to call it a "renewed" way of looking, since the prince's manifesto advocates a return to principles:

> In all my efforts I have tried to make it clear that all these subjects suffer the same problems because they have become detached from important basic principles – the principles that produce the active state of balance which is just as vital to the health of the natural world as it is for human society. We call this active but

---

[27] Michell and Rhone 1991, page 129.
[28] Op. cit. It should not be overlooked that the passing of Shaykh Nazim al-Haqqani occurred on 7 May, the day between the 6th and 8th.

balanced state "harmony" and this book is dedicated to explaining how harmony works.[29]

He goes on to explain "how the grammar of harmony works" in terms of specifically Pythagorean principles, and traces the legacy of Pythagoras' teachings through Plato to the Sufis.[30] No doubt the shaykh's characterization of the book as "a way of life" recalls the view of Plato, that Pythagoras was above all else a teacher of a way of life.[31]

As I have indicated previously, Prince Charles Philip Arthur George is the namesake of Saint George, as well as of the "Once and Future King." This Duke of Cornwall[32] is also named for his father Prince Philip, the Duke of Edinburgh who was born on the island of Corfu; and given this Greek context, he shares the attribute of "son of Philip" with Alexander the Great.[33] No doubt his participation in the legacy of Pythagoras contributes to his promise of becoming a true "philosopher king" in the

---

[29] HRH The Prince of Wales with Tony Juniper and Ian Skelly, *Harmony: A New Way of Looking at Our World*, New York: HarperCollins, 2010, page 5.

[30] Ibid., pages 97 ff. He includes the story of Pythagoras and the blacksmith with a picture of the tomb of Mevlana Rumi following a few pages after, though he does not openly refer to the story of Rumi and the goldsmith.

[31] This very legacy has been associated with one of the schools of Islamic philosophy, that of the *Ishraqiyyin*, a name that refers to the rising Sun (cf. Seyyed Hossein Nasr, *Three Muslim Sages*, Delmar: Caravan Books, 1976, page 62); this name also recalls the "solar illumination" mentioned earlier in connection with the language of Adam. In terms of a spiritual legacy, it is important to acknowledge that the Greatest Master of Islamic esoterism is sometimes called Ibn Iflatun, the "Son of Plato."

[32] His title of duke further recalls the early designation of Arthur as *dux bellorum*.

[33] This attribute has been made even more explicit in the example of Prince Charles' grandson, since Prince George *Alexander* Louis is the son of Prince William Arthur *Philip* Louis.

sense of Plato. Since the publication of *Harmony*, the prince has remained strong in his resolve to be a defender of nature, highlighting the wisdom of North American Indians in this regard.[34]

The relevance of environmental imbalance to our subject may in fact be glimpsed in a facet of folklore reported by the Brothers Grimm in their *Deutsche Sagen*. Once when a shepherd was brought into the Kyffhäuser, the emperor, no longer sleeping, stood up and asked, "Are ravens still flying around the mountain?" The shepherd's answer in the affirmative signalled that the time had not yet come for his emergence.[35] The implication is that when the natural order is sufficiently upset, the world will be ready for a renewal from the Unseen.

---

[34] Most recently, HRH announced the "Terra Carta," a contract to encourage private investment to be friendly with nature, and it is telling that the prince should so blatantly evoke the Magna Carta. Contemporary with the reign of Frederick II, this contract increased freedoms for the wealthy at the expense of the monarchy; and since these freedoms have led to the abuse of nature, justice demands that the future monarch should in turn call for a limit on these freedoms.

[35] There is a belief in England that ravens must be kept at the Tower of London or else the kingdom will fall; the resonance with the Germanic story is certainly striking, and suggests the English tradition is not as "invented" as researchers suppose. During World War II, only one raven remained at the tower, so Churchill ensured that the number was increased.

10

The Imperial Triangle

Qur'anic commentators agree that al-Khidr appears in the 18th chapter, even though he is not named. This chapter, entitled "The Cave," represents the arithmetical midpoint of the total number of words in the holy book. It also contains, as its title indicates, the story of the Companions of the Cave. The chapter includes several principal elements, beginning with the story of the Sleepers. The meeting of Moses and al-Khidr is related just past the middle of the chapter, and this is immediately followed by episodes from the story of Dhul-Qarnayn. In his scholarship concerning the Sleepers, Louis Massignon includes Traditions that indicate this chapter as having special relevance for a world out of balance, since it is identified as providing protection from the great parody called the Antichrist.[1] Though al-Khidr is not named, it is worth remembering that the Chapter of the Cave is not the only place the Green Man and Dhul-Qarnayn are associated, since in the Islamic versions of the Alexander Romance, al-Khidr is the companion and guide of Iskandar Dhul-Qarnayn. They are especially linked in the quest for that most sacred of springs that flows with the Water of Life.

---

[1] According to Islam, the most identifying physical characteristic of the Antichrist is that he has but one functioning eye, which serves to indicate a lack of balanced vision.

Iskandar Dhul-Qarnayn and al-Khidr in the Land of Darkness

If we consider the Qur'anic account of Dhul-Qarnayn, we discover that paths of the Sun provide the very framework for his story:

> *84. Lo! We made him strong in the land and gave unto every thing a road.*
> *85. And he followed a road*
> *86. Till, when he reached the setting place of the Sun, he found it setting in a muddy spring, and found a people thereabout: We said: O Dhul-Qarnayn! Either punish or show them kindness.*
> *87. He said: As for him who doeth wrong, we shall punish him, and then he will be brought back unto his Lord, who will punish him with awful punishment!*
> *88. But as for him who believeth and doeth right, good will be his reward, and We shall speak unto him a mild command.*
> *89. Then he followed a road*
> *90. Till, when he reached the rising place of the Sun, he found it rising on a people for whom We had appointed no helper therefrom.*
> *91. So (it was). And We knew all concerning him.*
> *92. Then he followed a road*
> *93. Till, when he came between the two mountains, he found upon their hither side a folk that scarce could understand a saying.*
> *94. They said: O Dhul-Qarnayn! Lo! Gog and Magog are spoiling the land. So may we pay thee tribute on condition that thou set a barrier between us and them?*

In the context of solar paths, the words of verses 86-88 recall especially the Pythagorean doctrine with its concern for the fate of souls. The example of the Saint Michael and Apollo alignment indicates a path belonging to the summer solstice sunset, while the archangel's iconography and the scales of Britain relate to judgment; here, in the direction of sunset, judgment belongs to Dhul-Qarnayn. Not unlike the solsticial gateways, the "two mountains" in verse 93 clearly recall mythological formulations of the gate through which the Sun enters and exits this world, the most ancient literary example of which is the twin-peaked Mount Mashu of the Epic of Gilgamesh.[2] These verses are followed by the episode with Gog and Magog and the construction of the Barrier of Alexander, but since we have already considered these matters in *Mysteries of Dune*, we need not focus on them here. Concerning the demonic forces beyond the barrier, it is perhaps enough to recall that the "gate of men" in the Classical world was alternatively known as *janua inferni*, the "Gate of Hell." In opposing such forces, Dhul-Qarnayn shares a function with Saint Michael especially, and indeed Lightning, the name of Alexander's sword, recalls the flaming sword of the archangel. It should not escape our notice that, given the environmental catastrophe unleased by modern humanity, the demonic activity mentioned here is that of "spoiling the land."

In the course of the foregoing, some attention was given to how the figure of Frederick II, among all the Holy Roman Emperors of the West, embodied a kind of inheritance from Alexander the Great. The Ottomans, who came to rule East Rome at the end of the Middle Ages, mirrored this inheritance but embraced it to an even greater degree. This inheritance was formulated in the Arabic title *sahib ul-qiran*, the "Owner of the Fortunate Conjunction." The word *qiran* shares its root with *qarn*, the word for "horn," but here the word relates to celestial conjunctions of the highest order. Certain rulers are recognized as embodying or owning this power on Earth

---

[2] This gateway is guarded by scorpion beings in the Epic of Gilgamesh, which recalls the role of Scorpio in the landscape of the mound builders. For that matter, Modoc mythology includes an otherworldly abode of the Sun related to the solar paths, and Mount Shasta has two peaks. Corfu, through which the solsticial alignment passes, literally signifies the "City of the Peaks," since the Old Fortress was built upon a rocky prominence with two peaks.

in different periods. Alexander the Great was regarded as the Sahib ul-qiran of his time, and in the Ottoman period, Sultan Sulaiman, recognized as the "Magnificent" in the West, was especially hailed as a Second Alexander and the Sahib ul-qiran.[3] One proof of his rank was the acquisition of a treasure that had formerly belonged to Alexander, the Jām-i Jamshid or "Cup of Jamshid."[4] Ottoman painting depicts the sultan holding the cup fashioned from a single ruby; yet even more wondrous was its supposed power to show its owner the affairs of the seven climates.[5] Perhaps not surprisingly, Sultan Sulaiman was believed by many to be the Qutb.

The octagonal monuments built by Frederick II in Italy mark the midpoint of the European alignment, yet as we have seen, the Castel del Monte counterbalances the northern position of Mount Gargano and its watchtower by its more southerly position. However, one aspect of this rather isolated location is that it matches the latitude of the Ottoman Imperial capital of Constantinople. Again, the Serpent Column of Delphi displays a bond with the Pythian Apollo, and the Ottomans preserved the monument in its position of honor. More than this, on the subject of Ottoman rule, it has been perceived that "its

---

[3] Cf. Cornell H. Fleischer, "The Lawgiver as Messiah: The Making of the Imperial Image in the Reign of Süleymân," *Soliman Le Magnifique et son Temps*, Paris: La Documentation Française, 1992. As the tenth ruler of the Ottoman house in the tenth century of the Islamic calendar, Sultan Sulaiman was regarded as the "Perfector of the Perfect Number," a particularly Pythagorean formulation (Lord Kinross, *The Ottoman Centuries*, New York: HarperCollins, 1977). On the Ottomans, however, it would be better to consult *Lords of the Horizons* by Jason Goodwin, the son of John Michell (New York: Picador, 1998).

[4] The name of this mythological king is formed of two terms: "Jam," from Yima, a chthonic king of ancient Iran, and "shid," meaning the Sun.

[5] Cf. Esin Atil, *Süleymanname: The Illustrated History of Süleyman the Magnificent*, New York: Abrams, 1986, pages 215-7.

nearest ideal analogue is found in the *Republic* of Plato,"[6] and so in the heritage of the Mysteries of Apollo. Be that as it may, if the solar path suggested by the specific orientation of the Castel del Monte is followed to the environs of Delphi, and specifically to the southern slopes of sacred Mount Parnassus, it may be seen that this position is equidistant from Constantinople and the octagonal Castel. Given that the alignment to the monument from Parnassus corresponds with the azimuth of the summer solstice sunset, it follows that a line from Parnassus to Constantinople corresponds to that of the summer solstice sunrise.

In a sense, this position near Mount Parnassus has been prefigured in the legendary account of Apollo walking to the Greek center of the world from the Vale of Tempe, since this valley is in fact due north of the point under consideration. This north-south axis may be extended in order to arrive at the midpoint of a line drawn between Castel del Monte and Constantinople. Obviously this line corresponds to the azimuth of sunrise and sunset on the equinoxes.[7] Considered together, the equinoctial and solsticial solar alignments form a balanced triangle, and given the Imperial connotations of its points, it might be referred to as the "Imperial Triangle." In any case, a number of symbolic relationships present themselves in relation to this geometrical figure upon the map, as in figure 8.

The historical emergence of Alexander the Great, for instance, proceeds from the land within this figure. In addition, the southward pointing of the triangle serves to direct our attention to the oasis of Siwa in Africa, where

---

[6] Albert Howe Lybyer, *The Government of the Ottoman Empire in the Time of Suleyman the Magnificent*, Cambridge: Harvard University Press, 1913, page 45.

[7] If this line is extended beyond Constantinople to the east, the alignment reaches the region of Ardanuç in the Caucasian borderlands, where the cup of the solar king Jamshid was claimed by the Ottomans.

Alexander consulted the oracle of Zeus Ammon. In accordance with the title Dhul-Qarnayn, Alexander came to be represented on coins with the horns of a ram, a chief attribute of Zeus Ammon. Indeed Alexander the Great was recognized as a son of Zeus, and so in this he compares with Apollo. There is a curious account of his visit to the oracle of Apollo at Delphi, which relates to the point of the triangle near Mount Parnassus that is the place of balance for the solsticial alignments.[8] Seeking to be recognized by the Pythia, the conqueror was told to come back later; Alexander responded by dragging the oracle out by the hair, only to let her go when she reassured him of his invincibility. In the context of Delphi, this violence might be compared to the slaying of Pytho by Apollo; yet Alexander is not replacing an old custodian of a sacred center with another. In this respect, the cleansing of the Temple in Jerusalem of the money changers comes to mind, especially in relation to Jesus' reported saying, "Think not that I am come to destroy the Law, or the prophets: I am not come to destroy, but to fulfill."[9]

The north-south axis through the environs of Tempe symbolically traces the steps of the Hyperborean Apollo, and it is equipoised between East Rome and the greatest monument of the western Emperor. In the Imperial Triangle, just as the summer solstice is symbolically associated with the south, we find the summer solstice alignments proceeding from the southern point of this axis; comparable lines indicating the winter solstice sunrise and sunset may therefore be plotted from its

---

[8] Recall that the teachings of the Seven Sages of Greece were displayed in the Temple of Delphi, whereas in Islamic accounts Iskandar is counseled by the "Seven Sages."

[9] Matthew 5:17. Jesus and Alexander might be compared for other reasons: both their historical lives lasted but 33 years; and while Jesus is absent from his tomb, it is indeed the entire tomb of Alexander the Great that is absent from the stage of history.

The Imperial Triangle

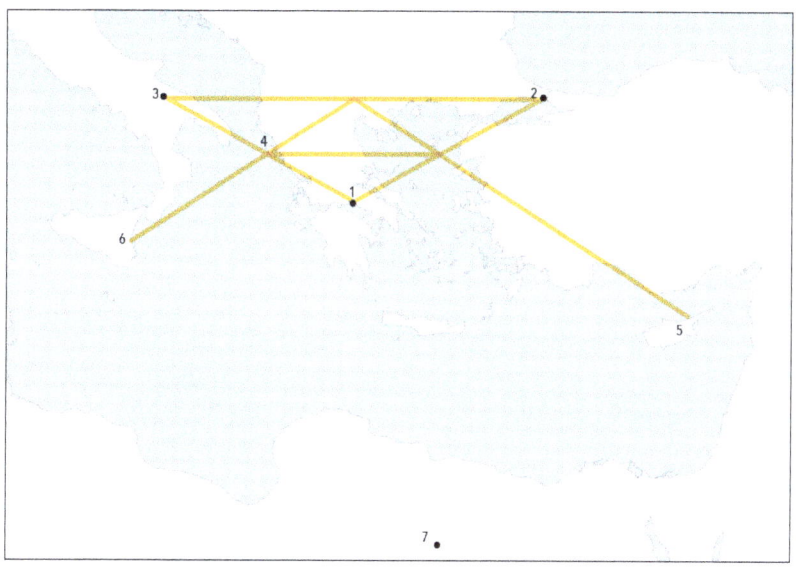

1	Southern flank of Mount Parnassus
2	Constantinople (Istanbul/Islambul)
3	Castel del Monte
4	Corfu
5	Cyprus
6	Sicily
7	Siwa

Figure 8
The Imperial Triangle

northern point. In figure 8, we see that the alignment of the winter solstice sunset reaches to the island of Sicily, while the alignment of the winter solstice sunrise reaches the island of Cyprus. The winter solstice is termed the "gate of gods," but it is also called *janua coeli*, the "Gate of Heaven," and it will be recalled that this gate allows passage for a spiritual elect.

Cyprus is the place of birth and passing of Shaykh Nazim al-Haqqani and is now the location of his tomb. There is a website managed from the island containing a vast library of his recorded teachings, mostly in video format, titled "Saltanat: Honorable Statements for the Honour of Adam's Children by Sheikh Muhammad Nazim al Haqqani ar Rabbani." This site was in fact established during his lifetime, and according to his instructions, the heading of the home page depicts two images flanking the title: to the left, a painting of the conqueror Mehmet II with his spiritual master Ak Shamsuddin[10] during the Ottoman entry into Constantinople; and to the right, the Holy Roman Emperor Frederick II. Despite the universal message contained in the wording of the site's title, the portrait of the Baptized Sultan was not universally understood by the Shaykh's followers. It scarcely needs to be explained how closely this heading mirrors the composition of the "Imperial Triangle" on the landscape of Europe, or at least its points to the east and west.

Cyprus has very early links both to the religions of Christianity and Islam. Regarding the former, mention was made above to the removal of the tomb of Saint Spyridon before its final placement in Corfu. Even so, there remains a tomb on Cyprus belonging to one of the earliest disciples of Christianity, Saint Barnabas. Since the challenge of Arianism figures especially in the hagiography of Spyridon, it is worth mentioning that the

---

[10] The spiritual lineage traced to this shaykh was called the Shamsi or "Solar" order.

apocryphal "Gospel of Barnabas" insists on Jesus' subordination to the Father, and so demonstrates a view comparable to that of Arius. Cyprus also figures in a curious tradition from an Arabic source relating to the Last Days of the world, concerning a mysterious book called the *Haqiqat al-injil* or "Truth of the Gospel" that could not be read when it was discovered in Spain, since its script was unknown.

> The Virgin Mary said that a council should be held on the island of Cyprus, and that God would put forward a shy and frail man at the end of time there who will address this council and who will explain what [the said book] contains. He will be accepted by all, and they will do as he tells them to…[11]

In 2010, Pope Benedict XVI visited Cyprus, and the supreme pontiff was embraced by Shaykh Nazim al-Haqqani in an unofficial meeting. Within three years, Benedict XVI became the first pope since the 13th century to resign his position willingly.

As for Sicily, the fate of Frederick II is mysteriously bound to Mount Etna, where "five thousand horsemen" were seen to escort him into the earth until the time of his return. This detail of a force of "five thousand" appears in the Holy Qur'an as a formulation of the angelic help that is yet available to the believers, and this detail appears all the more remarkable since a force of three thousand had already been seen as "armed horsemen"[12] at the Battle of Badr, the principal struggle during the founding of Islam. The notion of angelic help would seem to be out of place in the setting of the volcanic Mount Etna, the name of which in Arabic is *Jabal al-Nār*, the

---

[11] Ahmad Ibn Qāsim al-Hajari, *Kitāb Nāsir al-Dīn `Ala'l-Qawm al-Kāfirīn (The Supporter of Religion Against the Infidels)*, translated by Van Koningsveld et al., Madrid: CSIC/AECI, 1997, page 273.
[12] III, 124-5.

Mountain of Fire. In Arabic, the word for fire, *nār*, shares its root with the word for spiritual light, *nūr*, and we have already witnessed in the example of flaming swords that fire may very well be associated with spiritual power. Mount Etna is in fact the mythological location of the forges of Hephaestus, the divine smith, and René Guénon has explained that even though a malefic aspect often predominates in chthonic symbolism, the "subterranean fire" may have a luminous aspect as well.[13] No doubt the example of the Seven Sleepers as a formulation of the Abdal exemplifies this latter aspect, and this is likewise true in the case of the legend placing Emperor Frederick in Mount Etna.

The restoration of this luminous symbolism that has become overshadowed belongs above all to a time in which the state of things must be reversed. In the Imperial Triangle as it appears on the map, if another equinoctial line is drawn between the points where the winter solstice alignments cross the summer solstice alignments, we create a recognizable form, albeit flattened. This form is the geometrical representation of what is presented in the article "The Mountain and the Cave" by René Guénon; even more importantly, it has provided the basis for the posthumous transmission of his esoteric teachings through a particular formulation of the "Science of Letters."[14] Regarding its geometry, he explains that the upward pointing triangle represents the mountain, while the smaller, downturned triangle within the other signifies the cave (figure 9).

---

[13] Guénon 1972, page 189.
[14] Guénon 2004. On the so-called "Triangle of the Androgyne," see Vâlsan, op. cit., and Gilis, *Les Sept Étendards du Califat*, Paris: Éditions Traditionnelles, 1993, chapter XXIV. Curiously, this symbol has entered the popular consciousness in recent years as the mystical "Triforce" from a successful series of video games.

The Imperial Triangle

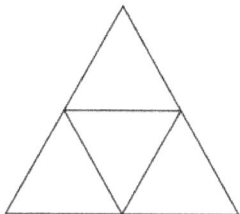

Figure 9
The Mountain and the Cave

Obviously, triangles, mountains, and cave have all figured prominently in this study; and the presence of Mount Parnassus here seems to perfectly support this symbolism. On the map, however, the figure is reversed.[15] Yet if the cave triangle has become the dominant shape, this must be seen here in the context of the emergence of the Sleepers from their cave. What had been hidden becomes apparent, so in a manner of speaking, the cave becomes the mountain apparent to all.

In the language of Islamic eschatology, this reversal is formulated as the Sun rising in the west, and so also in the title of the "Western Sun" as it is applied to the expected al-Mahdi who, in Islamic terms, prepares the faithful for the Second Coming.[16] The return of Jesus to the far West is in keeping with this, but since Christian doctrine associates this Second Coming above all with the Judgment, it is even more important to recognize Britain's privileged role that is "poised in the divine balance, as it is said, which supports the whole world." In solar terms,

---

[15] Obviously there can be no question here of sinister inversion, or else such an interpretation should be applied to the perspective of the traditional Chinese, for example, whose maps were oriented with the south facing up.

[16] On the Mahdi as the Western Sun, see *The Red and the White*, chapter 9.

the "new age" beginning in Glastonbury corresponds to the renewal of the day at sunrise, and such is the promise also of sleepers awakening. Only the apocalyptic aspect of Glastonbury properly accounts for King Arthur awakening at Mount Etna, however, and Sicily is found on a western alignment from the Imperial Triangle. In a similar manner, the right and left of the imagery on the "Saltanat" website are reversed from where they might be expected, since the western Emperor is pictured on the right and the conquest of East Rome on the left.

Shaykh Nazim al-Haqqani refers to the Second Coming as the establishing of the "kingdom of Heavens on Earth."[17] In a sense, a geography relating to the Abdal reveals the Earth already conforming to the directions of Heaven, and so the recent discoveries of ancient paths of the Sun that resonate with eschatology should be included among the signs of this Kingdom. René Guénon alludes to these matters in a passage that it is worth quoting finally at length:

> A rectification will indeed have to take place, and this will only be possible precisely when the lowest point is reached; this relates to the secret of the "reversal of the poles." Moreover, this rectification will have to be prepared, even visibly, before the end of the present cycle; but this can only be done by one who, by uniting in himself the powers of Heaven and Earth, of East and West, will manifest outwardly, both in the domain of knowledge and of action, the twin sacerdotal and royal power that has been preserved across the ages in the integrity of its unique principle by the hidden keepers of the Primordial Tradition. But it would be vain to seek to learn at present just when and how such a manifestation will occur, and doubtless it will be

---

[17] Cf. *Alchemy in Middle-earth*, page 95.

very different from anything one could imagine; the "mysteries of the Pole" (*al-asrār-al-qutbāniyah*) are assuredly well guarded, and nothing will be known of them outwardly until the fixed time is accomplished.[18]

---

[18] *Principles of Initiation*, Ghent: Sophia Perennis, 2001, page 254. The very recent planetary conjunction (*qiran*) of Saturn and Jupiter on the winter solstice of 2020 was an astrological sign of the highest order, and yet it was not accompanied by the corresponding earthly manifestation that Guénon describes here, and this demonstrates that apocalyptic timing must by definition be unpredictable. Nevertheless, the celestial portent has now been accomplished; the last time such a close conjunction was visible was 1226, that is, one of the four years during which Emperor Frederick II wore the crown of Jerusalem.

Index of Names

Aachen 35, 68
Abaris 82
Abdal 56-60, 68, 95-7
`Abdullah Daghistani, Shaykh 90
Ablun/Belen/Belenus 22, 51, 82
Abraham 21, 36, 57, 59-60, 96
Abu Ma`shar al-Balkhi 40, 83
Adam, Prophet 80, 81, 96, 126
Ahmad Yesevi, Khwaja 61
Ajumawi 106-8
Ak Shamsuddin 126
Albania 54, 63, 80, 84
Albion 84
Alchemy 90
Alexander 75-6, 79, 113, 116, 118-9, 121-4
`Ali bin Abi Talib 7, 57, 110
Antichrist 118
Apollo 15, 20-33, 35, 37, 40, 44, 47, 49, 51, 55, 58, 61, 72-3, 76, 82, 84, 88, 111-2, 114, 122-4
Arius 63, 127
Armageddon 94
Arthur, King 73, 77, 79-80, 84, 99, 102-3, 108, 116, 130
Athens 17, 21, 46, 67, 95

Atlantean 26, 84
Avebury 14, 114
Awtad 60, 112-4

Badr, Battle of 127
Bari 62-3, 65
Barnabas, Saint 126-7
Bektashi 54-5, 61, 90, 95
Beltane 14
Benedict XVI, Pope 127
Blake, William 7, 85, 109
Blois 17-8
Broadhurst, Paul 18, 47-8, 94
Burrowbridge Mump 82, 93

Cader Idris 83, 97-8
Cancer 28, 33-4
Capricorn 28, 33-4
Carmel, Mount 15-9, 41, 43-5, 47-50, 52, 81, 92, 94-5, 112
Carmelite 45
Castel del Monte 65-6, 69-74, 122-3, 125
Cautes 34
Cautopates 34
Celt 14, 19, 22, 24, 51, 82-5, 88, 92, 95
Chaldean 38, 83-4, 92
Charles, HRH The Prince of Wales 114-6

Index of Names

Channel Islands 94
Chartres 35
Cistercian 74
Companions of the Cave 61, 102-3, 118
Constantine, Emperor 29-30, 51, 63
Constantinople 51, 55, 122-3, 125-6
Corfu 17, 50, 52-3, 55, 62, 65, 80, 116, 125-6
Cornwall 16, 37, 48, 84-5, 87, 94, 102, 116
Cyprus 55, 89, 125-7

Dee, Dr. John 81, 90
Delos 17, 25-6, 44, 49-50, 92
Delphi 17, 20, 23-4, 26-9, 36-7, 44, 49-52, 55, 58-60, 69, 89, 92, 111, 122-4
Demir Baba 57-8, 84
Dhul-Fiqar 57, 110
Dhul-Qarnayn 75, 113, 118-21, 124
Diodorus 25-6, 82
Dome of the Rock 71, 80-1
Druid 81-3, 85, 87

Edinburgh 96-8, 116
Eildon Hills 73, 77
Elijah, Saint 41, 43-4, 79-80, 85, 95, 111-4
England 7, 12, 14, 16, 37, 67, 81, 89-90, 114, 117
Etna, Mount 77, 127-9
Evliya Çelebi 56, 61-2, 67, 86

Feng Shui 13
Fibonacci 71
Foggia 71-2
Francis, Saint 36, 70, 111
Franciscan 77
Frederick Barbarossa, Emperor 79
Frederick II, Emperor 69-72, 74, 76-7, 79-81, 103, 117, 121-2, 126-8, 131

Gargano, Mount 15, 17, 35-7, 48, 50-2, 55, 62, 64-5, 67-9, 86, 94, 109-2, 122
George, Saint 58, 113-4, 116
Gilis, Charles-André 23-4, 59, 128
Glastonbury 14, 71, 78, 81-3, 85-90, 93-5, 97-100, 102-3, 105, 106, 108-9, 114, 129
Göbekli Tepe 83
Gog and Magog 120-1
Götze, Heinz 71-2
Grail 76, 88-9
Gwyn Ap Nudd 83

Hasan, Imam 110
Haq 100, 103
Helios 18, 22, 26, 31, 33, 37, 40, 43
Hephaestus 128
Hermes 40, 47, 83
Hidrellez 57, 113
Hippolytus 33
Husayn, Imam 110
Hyperborean 24-6, 33, 37-9, 80, 82-4, 88, 101, 112, 124

Ibn 'Arabi, Shaykh Muhyiddin 19, 60, 96
Ibrahim, Prophet see Abraham
Idris 39-41, 47, 83-5. 96-7, 111-2
Ilyas, Prophet see Elijah, Saint
Imams 41, 45, 85
Indracht, Saint 86-7

133

Ireland 47, 84, 86, 92
'Isa, Prophet see Jesus Christ
Ishraqiyyin 116
Iskandar, see Alexander

Jabir bin Hayyan 100
Jami, `Abdur-Rahman 60
Jamshid 122-3
Jesus Christ 19, 63, 85-7, 89-90, 94, 96-7, 112, 124, 127, 129
John the Baptist, Saint 69, 112, 114
Joseph of Arimathea, Saint 85, 88

Kabbani 101, 113
Kalandar 56, 61, 102
Kantorowicz, Ernst 70, 75-6, 79
Karneios 25, 84, 88
Khidr 111, 113-4, 118-9
Kronos 21, 25, 101

Leys 13, 15, 29, 106
Livorno 67
Lucera 65, 71

Mandelbaum, Lukas 16, 35-7, 70
Maltwood, Katharine 81, 85
Mashu, Mount 121
Massignon, Louis 102-3, 118
Mecca 21, 23-4, 26
Mehmet the Conqueror, Sultan 126
Melchizedek 39
Mercury 10, 40, 47
Metatron 38-9, 52, 56, 60, 74-5, 111-2
Mevlevi 46
Michael, Saint 14-6, 19, 35-40, 43, 49, 51-2, 54-5, 60, 62, 74, 76, 87-8, 99. 110-11, 114, 121
Michell, John 8, 12, 15, 21, 27, 81, 85-6, 109, 114
Milky Way 33-4, 45, 105-6
Miller, Hamish 18, 47-8, 94
Mithra/Mitra 31, 33, 36-8
Mithras 31-5, 37, 39-41, 47
Mizan 100
Modoc 107-8, 112, 121
Moses 96-7, 118
Mound builders 105, 121
Mousa 97-8
Muhammad, Prophet 32, 57, 59, 63, 71, 80, 86, 111, 113
Musa, Prophet see Moses

Naqshbandi 60-1, 89-90, 101, 113
Nazim `Adil al-Haqqani, Shaykh 89-91, 95, 99, 100-1, 105, 109, 115, 126-7, 130
Nelson 95, 98
Nicholas, Saint 62-4
Norman 70, 81

Ogbourne St George 93, 115
Omphalos 21, 24, 32, 89
Otman Baba 57, 60, 95

Parnassus, Mount 23, 123-5, 129
Patrick, Saint 85-6
Pendle 95, 97
Perseus 33
Plato 27, 45, 116-7, 123
Plutarch 22, 49, 101
Pole Star 24, 27, 99
Porphyry 27, 32-4, 44, 83, 106
Pythagoras 13, 27, 33, 42, 44-6, 74, 82-3, 100, 116

Index of Names

Pytheas of Massalia 101
Pythia 22, 24, 124
Python 23, 29, 51

Qutb 41, 45, 60-1, 84-5, 101, 103, 109, 111, 122, 130

Rhodes 17-8, 44, 69
Richer, Jean 15, 21, 26, 28-9, 92
Richer, Lucien 15-6, 47, 92
Rome 19, 30-1, 47, 54, 56, 61, 95, 121, 124, 130
Rumi, Mevlana 14, 46, 89, 116

Sacra di San Michele 17, 37
Sa`d bin Abi Waqqas 86
Sahib ul-qiran 121-2
Saint Michael's Mount 16, 37, 47, 84, 93-4, 102
Saint-Michel, Mont 15-7, 36-7, 47, 51-2, 92-4
Saltanat website 126-30
Santiago de Compostela 45
Sari Saltik 54, 56-7, 59, 61-4, 67, 76, 80, 97
Scales (Libra) 99, 101
Science of Letters 80, 128
Scot, Michael 72, 74, 77, 79
Scotland 73, 96-99
Scott, Sir Walter 73
Serpent Column 29, 51, 122
Seven Sages of Greece 49, 124
Seven Spiritual Centers of Britain 95, 98-9, 101, 103, 115
Seven Sleepers of Ephesus, see Companions of the Cave
Shah-i Mardan, see `Ali bin Abi Talib

Shakespeare 29, 95
Shamsi 126
Shasta, Mount 106-7, 110, 121
Sicily 25, 70, 77, 79, 82, 125-7, 129
Siponto 36
Skellig Michael 47, 92-4
Sol 31, 33, 47
Solomon, Prophet-king 74
Spyridon, Saint 53, 55, 62-3, 126
Stonehenge 12-3, 26
Sulaiman the Magnificent, Sultan 122
Syria 26, 80-1

Tauroctony 32, 34
Tempe, Vale of 23, 55, 123-4
Teresa, Saint 45
Tombelaine 51
Tower of the Winds 46, 67, 73
Tolkien, J.R.R. 32
Tula 26, 101, 107

Ulansey, David 33-4
Ursa Major 27, 99, 101
Ursa Minor 99

Vâlsan, Michel 89, 96, 103, 128

Wales 12, 84, 97
Watkins, Alfred 13
William of Malmesbury 88
Windsor 95, 98, 114
Wotan 79

Yahya, Prophet see John the Baptist, Saint

Zeus 21, 24, 29, 124

www.ingramcontent.com/pod-product-compliance
Lightning Source LLC
Chambersburg PA
CBHW050033090426
42735CB00022B/3464